is a stimulating collection of twenty-five essays by outstanding contemporary writers. Statesmen, poets, anthropologists, critics, and scientists here express their personal views on many subjects, from the problems of young people to the exploration of outer space. Many provocative ideas are set forth which will sharpen the reader's own point of view about man in a complex world.

NED E. HOOPES is an Associate Professor of English at Pace College. Dr. Hoopes formerly taught at Evanston Township High School, Northwestern University, Harvard, Yale and Hunter College High School. He served as host on the television program *Reading Room*.

RICHARD PECK is the editor of two poetry anthologies, SOUNDS AND SILENCES and MINDSCAPES, both available from Dell. His own poems have appeared in Saturday Review and his articles have been published in many periodicals. Mr. Peck has taught at Hunter College and Hunter College High School in New York City, and was Assistant Director of the Council for Basic Education, Washington, D.C.

THE LAUREL-LEAF LIBRARY brings together under a single imprint outstanding works of fiction and nonfiction particularly suitable for young adult readers, both in and out of the classroom. This series is under the editorship of Charles F. Reasoner, Professor of Elementary Education, New York University.

Edge
of
Awareness

25 Contemporary Essays

edited by
Ned E. Hoopes
and Richard Peck

Published by Dell Publishing Co., Inc.
1 Dag Hammarskjold Plaza
New York, New York 10017
Copyright © 1966 by Dell Publishing Co., Inc.
All rights reserved
Laurel-Leaf Library ® TM 766734, Dell Publishing Co., Inc.

ISBN: 0-440-92218-6

First Printing—November, 1966
Second Printing—October, 1967
Third Printing—December, 1967
Fourth Printing—September, 1968
Fifth Printing—November, 1968
Sixth Printing—September, 1969
Seventh Printing—January, 1970
Eighth Printing—October, 1970
Ninth Printing—May, 1971
Tenth Printing—May, 1972
Eleventh Printing—July, 1973
Twelfth Printing—August, 1975
Thirteenth Printing—October, 1976
Fourteenth Printing—September, 1978

Printed in U.S.A.

Contents

ACKNOWLEDGMENTS

On Running Away by John Keats: Copyright © by John Keats. Reprinted by permission of The Sterling Lord Agency.

Alone on a Mountain Top by Jack Kerouac: Copyright © by Jack Kerouac. Reprinted by permission of The Sterling Lord Agency.

Old Man Facing Death by Oliver La Farge: Copyright © 1942 by Oliver La Farge. Reprinted by permission of Consuelo La Farge. Originally published in *The New Yorker.*

Portrait of Hemingway—Preface 1961 by Lillian Ross: Copyright © 1961, 1964 by Lillian Ross. Reprinted by permission of Simon and Schuster, Inc.

Real Women by Robert Graves: Reprinted from MAMMON AND THE BLACK GODDESS by Robert Graves, Doubleday & Company, Inc., Cassell & Company. Reprinted by permission of Willis Kingsley Wing. Copyright © 1963 by International Authors, N. V.

What I Believe by E. M. Forster: Copyright, 1939 by E. M. Forster. Reprinted from his volume TWO CHEERS FOR DEMOCRACY, by permission of Harcourt, Brace & World, Inc. and Edward Arnold (Publishers) Ltd.

Can We Survive the Fun Explosion by Joseph Wood Krutch: Reprinted by permission of Joseph Wood Krutch and *Saturday Review.*

Why I Dislike Western Civilization by Arnold Toynbee: Copyright © 1964 by The New York Times Company. Reprinted by permission. Reprinted by permission of Arnold Toynbee.

Fire Walking in Ceylon by Leonard Feinberg: Reprinted from *Atlantic Monthly.* Reprinted by permission of Evelyn Singer Agency.

One Vote for This Age of Anxiety by Margaret Mead: Reprinted by permission of Margaret Mead.

Eleanor Roosevelt: The Awakening by Archibald MacLeish: Copyright © 1965 by The New York Times Company. Reprinted by permission. Reprinted by permission of Archibald MacLeish.

Eulogy on Eleanor Roosevelt by Adlai E. Stevenson: "Her Journeys are Over" from LOOKING OUTWARD by Adlai E. Stevenson. Copyright © 1963 by Adlai E. Stevenson and Selma Schiffer. Reprinted by permission of Harper & Row, publishers. Excerpt from ACT FIVE and Other Poems by Archibald MacLeish reprinted by permission of Random House, Inc.

Introduction

Here is a group of nonfiction prose pieces for readers who enjoy examining important people's perspectives on various aspects of our contemporary and complex world. Each writer views similar and familiar experiences and circumstances from his own vantage point. By reading these twentieth-century essays, you can expand, clarify, and broaden your own point of view on these subjects.

These prose observations deal less with bare facts than with the relationship that exists among them. Each writer has his own special idea and his own individual slant; this focus is more important than the facts surrounding a problem. Though the nonfiction prose writer may find himself more closely bound to facts than his fiction-writing colleague, he is still more interested in evaluating the facts than in merely recording them. To each of these writers, the analysis of an experience is a far more stimulating subject than the experience itself.

Most of these essays have recently appeared in newspapers or magazines where the essayists of our time typically find the major outlet for expression. Here they can praise, complain, explain, reflect, plead, speculate, ridicule or comment.

The sixteenth-century French philosopher, Montaigne, was the first to call his short prose discussions *Essais*. His English contemporary, Francis Bacon, borrowed the title *Essays* for his collection of prose pieces. Later prose writers such as Milton and Voltaire expanded the essay form in their criticism of various aspects and institutions of their time. It was the eighteenth-century writers, such as Steele and Addison, who began to entertain as well as to instruct through essays published in weekly pamphlets. Such pamphlets as these are the direct ancestors of our modern-day periodicals.

Because nonfiction prose is rising steadily in popularity among modern readers, the collection you are about to read explores a vast range of subjects of vital interest—from the adventures and problems of young people to the frontiers and miracles of modern science. Many of the ideas you are about to encounter will give you new viewpoints upon much that makes living in the twentieth century an exciting challenge—a challenge not only to survival, but to appreciation.

James Froude, an historian of the last century, once wrote, "Human improvement is from within outwards." This idea has provided the focus for these essays—man's need to understand himself and therefore others, man's quest for his role in society and his admiration for those who have found and filled their roles with distinction, man's search for outlets of expression and appreciation, and man's hope for a better world through the fusion of science and art.

Even in our vastly complicated civilization, man must still be the measure of things, and his perceptions and beliefs are still the bases of life. Computing machines must free man to think, not rob him of thought; paintings and music and literature are meant to benefit man, not to baffle him; science must be a servant, not a master. Therefore, you will meet a great many stimulating people in these pages: statesmen, critics, poets, historians, the great woman who became a president's wife, an explorer who ventures to the bottom of the sea, a writer who becomes a fire-watcher, and many, many more people whose estimations of life will enrich your own.

—RICHARD PECK
NED E. HOOPES

Defining
Oneself
and Others

On Running Away

by John Keats

An essayist recalls one of his own youthful experiences of self-discovery after embarking upon a cross-country adventure of rattling freight trains, hobo jungles, and skid rows which led to an unexpected destination.

Ralph and I considered the possibility of police pursuit. We briefly debated the advisability of disguises. We decided that the wisest course was to try to postpone pursuit. To that end, we would tell our parents that we had each been invited by the other boy's family to spend the summer in Michigan. We made our secret plans, and one afternoon, shortly after high-school graduation, we uttered our little lies and headed for the railroad yards. That evening, while our families were no doubt discovering that neither owned a summer camp in Michigan, we were already far from our comfortable New Jersey suburb, rattling west across America. Our object was to get to China to join the American Volunteer Group in its aerial combat against the Japanese.

Two weeks later America was still rattling past, but now there was not a tree or house in sight. We slid the boxcar door wide open at dawn to see a vast prairie, pale gold in the east, dark in the west. Mountaintops shone above the shadows as they caught the first light. We were lonely, stiff from sleeping on a jittering wooden floor, cold, and tired of eating canned dog food. I have a clear memory of that morning in the morning of my life, now more than a quarter century ago. I can see in mind's eye those empty distances, and feel again that emptiness inside me. I am certain that Ralph was as fearful as I that day, but we did not admit our misgivings to each other. That would have been as much an admission of failure as returning home.

As we sat in the open doorway, watching the day brighten and the Rockies draw slowly nearer, I reflected on the recent past. No small part of the charm of running away from home lay in the presumption that the world was full of dangers. Naturally, we were eager to encounter them. Nothing was more pleasant than to imagine returning home as bronzed soldiers of fortune, bearing interesting scars and laden with the gifts of a grateful Chinese government. En route to the wars we would, of course, slay the usual number of local dragons. We were not running away from life but into it. We were sure that what we had left behind was lifeless. Our New Jersey suburb was pudgy with Buicks and Packards; a thing of clean linen, toothbrushes, electric razors, the once-a-week sound of the maid running the vacuum cleaner, and the empty conversations of soft-bellied people who worked in offices and played bridge and went to Bermuda in the spring.

Our view of ourselves, now that we rode boxcars and rolled our own cigarettes, was that we were tough. We wore blue denims, and soot from the coal-burning trains was ground into our clothing and our skin. Our adolescent stubble always seemed to be three days old. The men we now met were, for the most part, illiterate. The only woman we had seen on the trains had been a moron who was the chattel of a man who offered her to us for a dime each. One of the boys we had met was a male prostitute bound for Los Angeles. Two of the men in the gondola ahead of us looked to be thieves. There was no question about it: we were seeing Life. Unfortunately, it only too closely resembled the one we had left.

I could not help thinking, as we clacked along, that we knew of two thieves at home. One was a member of Rotary; the other, a minister's son. How was the man with the moron different from the parents who haunted summer hotels in perpetual hope of selling their unattractive daughters into matrimony? One of our high-school classmates had been established in a New York apartment by a successful businessman. The difference between that boy and the one headed for Los Angeles was that one moved in wealthier—I almost said better—circles. I have said that Ralph and I were inwardly fearful, but I should make clear that what was secretly feared was that life would prove not challenging but merely dull. In fact, we were finding it not only dull but dirty.

There were perils, but they were largely mechanical. For instance, one of our fellow passengers, an elderly nondescript, had made the mistake of dozing in the sunlight near the forward edge of a boxcar roof. When the cars banged together as the fast freight began to brake, clattering down the long hill into Cheyenne, the first sudden lurch tossed him forward, off the roof and under the wheels, which instantly bisected him. One night when Ralph and I sheltered from the rain in a sort of cave formed by overhanging boards piled on a flatcar, we narrowly escaped a similar fate when the load shifted as we rounded a curve. Stupidity, we realized, was lethal. But where were the unknown dangers with which the world was supposedly replete? Specifically, where were the toughs and murderers who, in the public mind, so thickly populated the hobo jungles and the Hoovervilles?

We met none. The well-fed burghers of our hometown, to whom the Depression was more of a nuisance than a catastrophe, regarded the scarecrows of the Hoovervilles as dubiously as a French marquis might have looked on a Parisian mob in 1790, but they were wrong. At least in the West, the hobo jungles were merely unofficial public campsites tenanted by a slowly changing population of migrants down on their luck. Feeling a need for government, these men formed their own. Many were veterans of World War I, and in camp after camp a former sergeant was elected or appointed leader. He greeted new arrivals, assigned them huts or sleeping space and explained the rules: *No fighting, thieves get beat up, you keep your place clean. And remember, try to bring back something for chow. Everybody brings something for chow.*

In the America of those days everyone understood everyone else's problem, because it was also his own. If a man could not find work in one town, he tried another. Having no money to spend for transportation, he thumbed rides (which those who had cars were glad to offer), or he hopped a freight (while brakemen looked the other way). The people on the road were not derelicts. The derelicts, then as now, lived in the Skid Rows of our cities. All the men and boys on the road, however modest their abilities and backgrounds, were looking for work. Some were bindle stiffs who had known nothing all their lives except stoop labor, moving forever from harvest to harvest. Others were genuine hobos—men who could work at nearly any trade, but whose free choice it was to hold no job long. All hobos said they intended to settle down someday, but not just yet. There was still a lot of country they wanted to see first. With rare exceptions, we met none but friends. Perhaps it is true that in good times no one takes to the road but the bad, but in our bad times we met virtually none but the good.

Ralph and I had looked for jobs wherever the trains stopped on our way through the Midwest, and while we found none, there were always housewives who would put their cares aside to consider ours. They would give us make-work so that we should not seem beggars. We would wash the windows, or whitewash the henhouse, or clean the yard or the rain gutters, and while we puttered, the woman would prepare us a meal. Often as not they would also give us a package of food to take to the train. In small towns everyone knew the train schedules, and sometimes we would be told, "Gracious, there *is* some work I do want done, but you boys won't have time for it before the train leaves, so why don't you just sit down and I'll try to find something in the icebox."

It was disappointing to be welcomed everywhere, when it was so important to us to learn whether we could make our unaided way through a violent world. Of course, we heard that the railroad detectives were the sadistic enemies of the tramp. We heard they loved nothing more than to beat a defenseless man insensible and toss his body on an outbound freight. The most famous of these detectives was one Green River Slim. Alas, we never saw a yard detective, and Green River Slim turned out to be just as imaginary, and as ubiquitous, as that other great American whose name was also found chalked upon a thousand boxcars (and who later would go to war)—Kilroy.

In retrospect it is clear to me that Ralph and I were the only people of our acquaintance on the road who were dangerous. We were looking for trouble; everyone else was looking for work. Our ambition was to kill Japanese for fun and money, and meanwhile prove to the world how tough we were. Nobody seemed to view us in just this light except, perhaps, a toothless old wreck, with breath like a vulture's, who accosted us outside a Skid Row bar in Chicago.

"Want to see how hard you can hit?" he asked us. "Gimme a quarter, I'll let you hit me. See can you knock me out."

He followed us for nearly a block, pleading, promising not to hit back, flattering us, and finally, when he saw it was no use, cursing. Looking back on it, I think we fled from him.

Novelty, rather than true discovery, entertained us to the foothills of the Rockies. It would be years before we learned the truth of Montaigne's remark that the traveler must take himself wherever he goes. Yet I do remember that our first sight of those mountains seemed a mockery; I remember the feeling of emptiness they created inside me. In themselves they were an enormous fact, and consideration of one fact led to a consideration of others. One was that no one wanted us to do anything for him except leave town; people were glad to help us on our way. Another was that we had nothing to offer anyone except manual labor, which was not in demand, or our money, which was. We had left home with two hundred dollars between us, all saved from the unearned money our families had allowed us. It had cost us thirty dollars to purchase blankets, denims, work shoes and sufficient dog food to carry us to South Dakota. Canned dog food recommended itself to us as the cheapest comestible to be had. It constituted a balanced diet, and was rather tasty—at first. The meals donated by housewives were occasional banquets, but as the trains rolled farther west and the towns thinned out, dog food became our staple, and it seemed that we might have to consume another one hundred and seventy dollars' worth of it if we could not immediately find a ship for China. I now suspect that what caused my feeling of emptiness was a premonition that one could not live without money, but that no one could earn money save at the loss of one's freedom. The world seemed a jail.

In the high Rockies, two boys our age boarded the train. They were Louis Wang, a Chinese-American of Fresno, and Phillip Benoff, a Russian-American from Los Angeles.

They had gone adventuring to the East Coast and now were returning to California; Phil to join the Army and Louis to join a gambling house where he would run a dice table. We told them of our plans, and they decided to come along with us instead. In that moment we became an army, and the world brightened considerably. Changed by the alchemy of a dream, the mountains' vast sterility was transformed into magnificence. We would sort the facts of life to suit ourselves. Crossing the Pacific would be no problem. Everyone knew that boys could get jobs as wipers to work a passage. Boys had been running away to sea for centuries. We had only to find a ship that needed four wipers.

Before it was over, we must have walked the docks of every port on the West Coast—including those of minor fishing towns. *Were we members of the union?* No. *Let's see your identification papers.* We had none.

Do you have passports? Passports?

We went to the union offices. *Buddy, we got 3,000 guys on the beach, and every single one of them is an Able Seaman.*

Ralph and I, blue-eyed and blond, went to Scandinavian shipping companies, saying, "Ay ban Swade. Ay yust want ship home." And they laughed and said they were sorry.

We persisted until someone finally told us the truth about the American Volunteer Group. It seemed that the volunteers had been carefully selected by the United States Government from its ranks of Army, Navy and Marine Corps pilots. We went to the recruiting offices, only to be told that we would need at least two years of college credits to qualify for the aviation-cadet programs. At this point, we all went to Fresno with Louis to think things over.

College was out of the question for Louis and Phil, but Ralph and I had only to ask to go, and our parents would send us. In Fresno I began to see the fallacy of our position: our confidence in ourselves had all along been based on the assumption that we were different from all other men: not on the slightest feeling of identity with mankind. This could not be helped; we were what our first eighteen years had made us. At any moment we could have walked out of the shacks of the hobo jungle to the nearest Western Union office, and hours later been dressed in decent clothes, sitting down to the best dinner in the best hotel of whatever town it was, while a hotel clerk booked reservations for us on the next Pullman headed for Newark, New Jersey. The difference between us and all others was, as Smollett would say, wholly matter-money. In the back of our minds we had always known this, and it was the source of our strength and the source of our great weakness; it made us hold something back in our relationships with others; we were never identifying with them; thus a barrier, built of dollars, shut us off from the kindness of Midwestern housewives, and from Louis and Phil. We and the other people on the road were of different tribes.

I do not mean to say that I worked all this out in so many words at age eighteen, sitting at the bar of a tacky one-story gambling house in Fresno, watching Chinese playing fan-tan and Americans shooting craps. I simply mean that I was then dimly but uneasily aware of what I am now saying. I remember that we did wonder aloud whether going back home to college would not be an admission of defeat, but that we rationalized our way to the view that the *only* path to war in the Chinese skies led through two years of college followed by an aviation-cadet program. This decided, we broke what had been a summer-long silence and wrote our first letters home.

The immediate answer was a large check, which we expected, and the utterly demoralizing news—which we had not expected at all—that our parents, confident that we would get over our silliness, had already entered us in college for the fall term. In those days not many colleges demanded College Entrance Examination Board test scores, but all of them had vacancies and most were willing to pretend that the customer was always bright.

Our parents' casual certainty about us was infuriating. We therefore determined upon one final gesture that would restore to us something of our romantic view of ourselves as hard, tough men. Louis Wang had a motorcycle. If he would let us borrow it, we would ride it east and send it back to him. Ralph's father owned a manufacturing concern (Ralph showed Louis the company letterhead) and Ralph would have the shipping department crate the motorcycle and send it back.

Oddly enough, Louis agreed. Perhaps he was intrigued by our idea of trying to drive across the continent without stopping except for gasoline. We all wondered if anyone had done this before; if it really could be done; if so, in how little time. So Louis showed us how to start and stop the thing, and we bought a pillow in a five-and-ten-cent store to wire onto the back fender to form a seat for the one who would not be driving. It would not take us long to learn how to drive it, Louis said. We shook hands and went blasting out of Fresno forever.

We raced furiously to Sacramento; scuttered over the mountains and into Reno with our backsides beginning to turn black and blue. We sped across the salt flats; paused for gasoline, coffee and a bottle of whiskey at a Wyoming town where all three were sold at the town's one store. Our headlights, at ninety miles an hour, suddenly illuminated white-faced Herefords wandering across an open range in Montana, and we went off the road to avoid them, shouting and scattering gravel and cattle; somehow wobbled back onto the road again and out of the herd. We gradually drew closer to what we believed to be the lights of a town, shining far ahead in the clear Western distances, only to realize at last that, in our grogginess, we were creeping nearer and nearer to the tailgate of an enormous, brightly lighted trailer truck. We drank black coffee at the next gas pump; coffee laced with whiskey. We also fell asleep while rounding a curve in Iowa. I remember seeing a shower of sparks, and eventually realizing they were caused by the foot peg grinding along the pavement while centrifugal force and an unbanked curve were keeping us alive. I shouted to Ralph to stop trying to show off, and he woke up suddenly, caught himself, and swerved back to our own side of the road.

Eighty hours after leaving Fresno we were streaking along the new Pennsylvania Turnpike at night, chased by police. They did not arrest us. They merely wanted to tell us the road was not yet open; that a thousand yards ahead was a place where the first bridge would be, when it was built. When we reached New Jersey we slept for two days, and it was some days later before the swelling left our hands and arms and the bruises faded from our buttocks.

Then, having nothing better to do, we went to college. We hated that. The boys and girls who went to college were nothing but tame kids who would unquestioningly evolve into the bridge players who made nonconversation. They joined fraternities, cheered at the games, did their homework, earned their grades, went to the dances and swung and swayed with Sammy Kaye; while we, in our arrogant innocence, looked derisively upon all this from an outside world. We were different. We were 6,000 miles by boxcar and motorcycle apart from them. We knew it, and they did too. Just to be sure they knew, we always rolled our own cigarettes on campus and dressed in our own sooty denim pants.

Looking back on it now, it seems odd to say we felt such a difference between ourselves and the college children, particularly when I have already said that we, in a formless way, had begun to suspect that the artificial differences between one man and another are inconsequential when compared to the real similarities that unite them. Moreover, Ralph and I were now back among our own kind. Why, then, the studied insolence of the Bull Durham and the dirty Levi's?

I suppose, now, that the pose and the costume were our own way of saying to other collegians, *You know nothing about it.* We would sit in economics class, and the others would brightly chatter with the young doctoral student who was our instructor, and I would slump back in my chair with my hands in my pockets, angry and silent, hearing nothing of this footless patter of cyclical depressions. Instead, I would see in my mind's eye a filling-station door open, and the woman in the man's coat and hat emerge, a scarf wrapped around her nose and mouth to keep out the driving dust; she would wad another protective rag around the nozzle of the hose and the opening of the gas tank to put two dollars' worth of gasoline into a wretched jalopy crowded with an empty-faced family of spindly children and bearing on its roof rug-wrapped bundles and the flat steel web of a cheap double bed, and hear the man ask whether, instead of paying the money, he could stay and work for two days.

An *ad hominem* approach to Economics 201A was not a certain path to success in the subject, but I cared nothing for the course and less for the grade. The feeling grew on me that no one in college, including the smug young instructors with the Phi Beta Kappa keys, knew what the devil he was talking about; that they were all playing at an intellectual game that insulted the dignity of experience.

This was not a feeling I could put into words at that time. I had only the unexpressed knowledge, sitting silent inside me, that there was no place for me then, or perhaps ever, in any world I did not make for myself. Indeed, in retrospect, this seems to have been the cardinal lesson of our summer's trip. It will be seen that Ralph and I failed to make our dream come true; that our first young research for the stuff of life proved only that we were not at home in either the suburban or the proletarian worlds. Nor were we at home in the academic world. In fact, we would never be at home in any patterned world. No one ever is. No matter how much we share with all mankind, each of us is bitterly alone. Our true distance from our neighbor begins to yawn when we at length discover the unexplored darkness within ourselves, and begin to understand that he who travels farthest and fastest into this darkness must travel alone; and that the ultimate destination of every traveler is always himself.

It was just this sense of the void within us that our trip had given us; it was our first, urgent command to get to work and fill the void; our summer trip provided us with our first inkling that our claims to identity would be entirely determined by our experience of ourselves.

In this sense, I can say that some part of me, now and forever, answers to the sounds of a train whistling lonely in the night, and to the deep tones of foghorns in the mists of the Northwestern coast. Some part of me is still a boy sweating at unloading watermelons from a truck in Portland; I am still shivering atop a cattle car in the winds driving through the snow-covered high passes. There is still in whoever I am the wink of campfires and the sight of the drunken man jumping across a fire and someone hitting him with a railroad spike and him falling into the fire. I can still see the lights of San Francisco and of Alcatraz from Coit Tower, and the delicate faces of the Chinese girls that Louis found for us. I have a memory of walking the docks in the rain in Seattle, and of sleepless nights in the fumigated cots of flophouses run by the Gospel Mission; of the Western wastelands creeping past and a hawk swooping on a gopher. Most clearly, I can see the faces of hopeful men who would never know anything other than disappointment, and the burst of spray against the rocks and among the tidal pools of Monterey. I remember lying on rattling floorboards at night, wondering whether I would wind up in jail, or whether any girl would ever want to marry me, and if I would ever see my family again. I have many memories, and if I am not sure yet what all of them mean, I am nonetheless certain that whoever I am is whatever my memories have made me; that I am becoming whatever I can find out about myself.

Nagging at my mind is Churchill's remark that "without a measureless and perpetual uncertainty, the drama of human life would be destroyed." I suppose that each of us, in his own way and at his own time, ventures as far as he chooses to dare in search of himself. Amy Lowell wondered, "Christ! What are patterns for?" They are largely for the timid; for those who find them comfortable. It seems to me that an adventure must be defined as an undertaking whose end it is impossible to know.

That is why I applaud the youthful dramatist, the would-be adventurer, who breaks the pattern, who with mounting excitement writes the farewell note and slips out the window at dead of night to set off afoot for the railroad yards to board a freight bound for California. I believe I know how he feels. More important, I know that he is not running away from something so much as he is running toward something: toward life; toward himself; toward an end that cannot be known.

I wish him well. His chances of finding what he seeks are never good, but they are at least better than the chances of those who stay at home, placidly accepting patterns they never made, or chose.

Alone on a Mountain Top

by Jack Kerouac

One of the first of the beat authors learned who he really is while isolated on Desolation Peak contemplating the silent grandeur of nature.

Anybody who's been to Seattle and missed Alaskan Way, the old waterfront, has missed the point. Here the totem-pole stores, the waters of Puget Sound washing under old piers, the dark gloomy look of ancient warehouses and pier sheds, and the most antique locomotives in America switching boxcars up and down the waterfront, give a hint, under the pure cloud-mopped, sparkling skies of the Northwest, of great country to come. Driving north from Seattle on Highway 99 is an exciting experience because suddenly you see the Cascade Mountains rising on the northeast horizon, truly *Komo Kulshan* under their uncountable snows. The great peaks covered with trackless white, worlds of huge rock twisted and heaped and sometimes almost spiraled into fantastic, unbelievable shapes.

All this is seen far above the dreaming fields of the Stilaquamish and Skagit valleys, agricultural flats of peaceful green, the soil so rich and dark it is proudly referred to by inhabitants as second only to the Nile in fertility. At Milltown, Washington, your car rolls over the bridge across the Skagit River. To the left—seaward, westward—the Skagit flows into Skagit Bay and the Pacific Ocean. At Burlington you turn right and head for the heart of the mountains along a rural valley road through sleepy little towns and one bustling agricultural market center known as Sedro Woolley with hundreds of cars parked aslant on a typical country-town Main Street of hardware stores, grain-and-feed stores and five-and-tens. On deeper into the deepening valley, cliffs rich with timber appearing by

the side of the road, the narrowing river rushing more
swiftly now, a pure translucent green like the green of
the ocean on a cloudy day but a saltless rush of melted
snow from the High Cascades . . . almost good enough to
drink north of Marblemount. The road curves more and
more till you reach Concrete, the last town in Skagit
Valley with a bank and a five-and-ten; after that the mountains rising secretly behind foothills are so close that now
you don't see them but begin to feel them more and more.

At Marblemount the river is a swift torrent, the work of
the quiet mountains. Fallen logs beside the water provide
good seats to enjoy a river wonderland. Leaves jiggling
in the good clean northwest wind seem to rejoice. The top-
most trees on nearby timbered peaks, swept and dimmed
by low-flying clouds, seem contented. The clouds assume
the faces of hermits or of nuns, or sometimes look like
sad dog acts hurrying off into the wings over the horizon.
Snags struggle and gurgle in the heaving bulk of the river.
Logs rush by at twenty miles an hour. The air smells of pine
and sawdust and bark and mud and twigs; birds flash over
the water looking for secretive fish.

As you drive north across the bridge at Marblemount
and on to Newhalem the road narrows and twists until
finally the Skagit is seen pouring over rocks, frothing, and
small creeks come tumbling from steep hillsides and pile
right in. The mountains rise on all sides, only their shoulders and ribs visible, their heads out of sight and now
snowcapped.

At Newhalem extensive road construction raises a cloud
of dust over shacks and cats and rigs; the dam there is the
first in a series that create the Skagit watershed which pro-
vides all the power for Seattle.

The road ends at Diablo, a peaceful company settlement
of neat cottages and green lawns surrounded by close-
packed peaks named Pyramid and Colonial and Davis.
Here a huge lift takes you one thousand feet up to the level
of Diablo Lake and Diablo Dam. Over the dam pours a jet
roar of water through which a stray log sometimes goes
shooting out like a toothpick in a one-thousand-foot arc.
Here for the first time you're high enough really to begin
to see the Cascades. Dazzles of light to the north show
where Ross Lake sweeps back all the way to Canada, open-

ing a view of the Mt. Baker National Forest as spectacular as any vista in the Colorado Rockies.

The Seattle City Light and Power boat leaves on regular schedule from a little pier near Diablo Dam and heads north between steep timbered rocky cliffs toward Ross Dam, about half an hour's ride. The passengers are power employees, hunters and fishermen and forestry workers. Below Ross Dam the footwork begins; you must climb a rocky trail one thousand feet to the level of the dam. Here the vast lake opens out, disclosing small resort floats offering rooms and boats for vacationists, and just beyond, the floats of the U. S. Forestry Service. From this point on, if you're lucky enough to be a rich man or a forest-fire lookout, you can get packed into the North Cascade Primitive Area by horse and mule and spend a summer of complete solitude.

I was a fire lookout and after two nights of trying to sleep in the boom and slap of the Forest Service floats, they came for me one rainy morning—a powerful tugboat lashed to a large corral float bearing four mules and three horses, my own groceries, feed, batteries and equipment. The muleskinner's name was Andy and he wore the same old floppy cowboy hat he'd worn in Wyoming twenty years ago. "Well, boy, now we're gonna put you away where we can't reach ya; you better get ready."

"It's just what I want, Andy, be alone for three solid months, nobody to bother me."

"It's what you're sayin' now, but you'll change your tune after a week."

I didn't believe him. I was looking forward to an experience men seldom earn in this modern world: complete and comfortable solitude in the wilderness, day and night, sixty-three days and nights to be exact. We had no idea how much snow had fallen on my mountain during the winter, and Andy said: "If there's not enough it means you gotta hike two miles down that hard trail every day or every other day with two buckets, boy. I ain't envyin' you. I been back there. And one day it's gonna be hot and you're about ready to broil, and bugs you can't even count 'em; and next day a li'l 'ole summer blizzard come hit you around the corner of Hozomeen—which sits right there near Canada in your back yard—and you won't be able to stick logs fast enough in that potbelly stove of yours." But I had a full rucksack loaded with turtleneck sweaters and warm shirts and pants and long wool socks bought on the Seattle waterfront, and gloves and an earmuff cap, and lots of instant soup and coffee in my grub list.

"Shoulda brought yourself a quart of brandy, boy," said Andy, shaking his head as the tug pushed our corral float up Ross Lake, through the log gate and around to the left dead north, underneath the immense rain shroud of Sourdough Mountain and Ruby Mountain.

"Where's Desolation Peak?" I asked, meaning my own mountain (*A mountain to be kept forever,* I'd dreamed all that spring).

"You ain't gonna see it today till we're practically on top of it," said Andy, "and by that time you'll be so soakin' wet you won't care."

Assistant Ranger Marty Gohlke of Marblemount Ranger Station was with us, too, also giving me tips and instructions. Nobody seemed to envy Desolation Peak except me. After two hours pushing through the storming waves of the long rainy lake with dreary, misty timber rising steeply on both sides and the mules and horses chomping on their feedbags, patient in the downpour, we arrived at the foot of Desolation Trail and the tugman (who'd been providing us with good hot coffee in the pilot cabin) eased her over and settled the float against a steep, muddy slope full of bushes and fallen trees. The muleskinner whacked the first mule and she lurched ahead with her double-sided pack of batteries and canned goods, hit the mud with fore-hoofs, scrambled, slipped, almost fell back in the lake and finally gave one mighty heave and went skittering out of sight in the fog to wait on the trail for the other mules and her master. We all got off, cut the barge loose, waved to the tugman, mounted our horses, and started up, sad and dripping, in the heavy rain.

At first the trail, always steeply rising, was so dense with shrubbery we kept getting shower after shower from overhead and from branches hit by our outjutting knees. The trail was deep, with round rocks that kept causing the animals to slip. At one point a great fallen tree made it impossible to go on until Old Andy and Marty went ahead with axes and cleared a shortcut around the tree, sweating and cursing and hacking, as I watched the animals. By and by they were ready, but the mules were afraid of the rough steepness of the shortcut and had to be prodded through with sticks. Soon the trail reached alpine meadows powdered with blue lupine everywhere in the drenching mists, and with little red poppies, tiny-budded flowers as delicate as designs on a tiny Japanese teacup. Now the trail zigzagged widely back and forth up the high meadow. Soon we saw the vast, foggy heap of a rock-cliff face above and Andy yelled, "Soon's we get up high as that we're almost there, but that's another two thousand feet, though you'd think you could reach up and touch it!"

I unfolded my nylon poncho and draped it over my head, and, drying a little, or, rather, ceasing to drip, I walked alongside the horse to warm my blood and began to feel better. But the other boys just rode along with their heads bowed in the rain. As for altitude all I could tell was from some occasional frightening spots on the trail where we could look down on distant treetops.

The alpine meadow reached to timber line, and suddenly a great wind blew shafts of sleet on us. "Gettin' near the top now!" yelled Andy. And now there was snow on the trail, the horses were chumping through a foot of slush and mud, and to the left and right everything was blinding white in the gray fog. "About five and a half thousand feet right now," said Andy, rolling a cigarette as he rode in the rain.

We went down, then up another spell, down again, a slow gradual climb, and then Andy yelled, "There she is!" and up ahead in the mountaintop gloom I saw a little shadowy peaked shack standing alone on the top of the world and I gulped with fear:

"This my home all summer? And *this* is summer?"

The inside of the shack was even more miserable, damp and dirty, leftover groceries and magazines torn to shreds by rats and mice, the floor muddy, the windows impenetrable. But hardy Old Andy, who'd been through this kind of thing all his life, got a roaring fire crackling in the potbellied stove and had me lay out a pot of water with almost half a can of coffee in it, saying, "Coffee ain't no good 'less it's *strong!*" and pretty soon the coffee was boil-

ing a nice brown aromatic foam and we got our cups out
and drank deep.

Meanwhile I'd gone out on the roof with Marty and removed the bucket from the chimney and put up the
weather pole with the anemometer and done a few other
chores; and when we came back in, Andy was frying
Spam and eggs in a huge pan and it was almost like a
party. Outside, the patient animals chomped on their supper bags and were glad to rest by the old corral fence
built of logs by some Desolation lookout of the thirties.

Darkness came, incomprehensible.

In the gray morning after they'd slept in sleeping bags
on the floor and I on the only bunk in my mummy bag,
Andy and Marty left, laughing and saying, "Well, what
ayou think now, hey? We been here twelve hours already
and you still haven't been able to see more than twelve
feet!"

"By gosh that's right, what am I going to do for watching fires?"

"Don't worry, boy, these clouds'll roll away and you'll
be able to see a hunnerd miles in every direction."

I didn't believe it and I felt miserable and spent the day
trying to clean up the shack or pacing twenty careful feet
each way in my "yard" (the ends of which appeared to
be sheer drops into silent gorges), and I went to bed
early. About bedtime I saw my first star, briefly, then giant
phantom clouds billowed all around me and the star was
gone. But in that instant I thought I'd seen a mile below
me gray-black Ross Lake where Andy and Marty were
back in the Forest Service boat which had met them at
noon.

In the middle of the night I woke up suddenly and my
hair was standing on end: I saw a huge black shadow in
my window. Then I saw that it had a star above it, and
realized that this was Mt. Hozomeen (8,080 feet) looking
in my window from miles away near Canada. I got up from
the forlorn bunk with the mice scattering underneath and
went outside and gasped to see black mountain shapes
gianting all around; and not only that but the billowing
curtains of the northern lights shifting behind the clouds.
It was a little too much for a city boy. The fear that the

Abominable Snowman might be breathing behind me in
the dark sent me back to bed where I buried my head inside my sleeping bag.

But in the morning—Sunday, July sixth—I was amazed
and overjoyed to see a clear blue sunny sky, and down
below, like a radiant pure snow sea, the clouds made a
marshmallow cover for all the world and all the lake
while I abided in warm sunshine among hundreds of miles
of snow-white peaks. I brewed coffee and sang and drank a
cup on my drowsy warm doorstep.

At noon the clouds vanished and the lake appeared below, beautiful beyond belief, a perfect blue pool twenty-
five miles long and more, and the creeks like toy creeks
and the timber green and fresh everywhere below and even
the fishing boats of vacationists on the lake and in the
lagoons. A perfect afternoon of sun, and behind the shack
I discovered a snowfield big enough to provide me with
buckets of cold water till late September.

I had taken this job so I could round up a little grub-
stake and take off for Mexico for a year, but also I wanted
to be alone on the top of a mountain and see what it was
like, and besides, all the mountain climbers and loggers
I'd known on the West Coast had told me not to miss the
High Cascades.

My job was to watch for fires. One night a terrific lightning storm made a dry run across the Mt. Baker National
Forest without any rainfall. When I saw that ominous black
cloud flashing wrathfully toward me I shut off the radio
and laid the aerial on the ground and waited for the worst.
Hiss! hiss! said the wind, bringing dust and lightning
nearer. Tick! said the lightning rod, receiving a strand of
electricity from a strike on nearby Skagit Peak. Hiss! Tick!
and in my bed I felt the earth move. Fifteen miles to the
south, just east of Ruby Peak and somewhere near Panther
Creek, a large fire raged, a huge orange spot. At ten o'clock
lightning hit it again and it flared up dangerously.

I was supposed to note the general area of lightning
strikes. By midnight I'd been staring so intently out the
dark window I got hallucinations of fires everywhere, three
of them right in Lightning Creek, phosphorescent orange
verticals of ghost fire that seemed to come and go.

In the morning, there at 177°16' where I'd seen the big

fire, was a strange brown patch in the snowy rock showing where the fire had raged and sputtered out in the all-night rain that followed the lightning. But the result of this storm was disastrous fifteen miles away at McAllister Creek, where a great blaze had outlasted the rain and exploded the following afternoon in a cloud that could be seen from Seattle. I felt sorry for the fellows who had to fight these fires, the smoke-jumpers who parachuted down on them out of planes and the trail crews who hiked to them, climbing and scrambling over slippery rocks and scree slopes, arriving sweaty and exhausted only to face the wall of heat when they got there. As a lookout I had it pretty easy and only had to concentrate on reporting the exact location (by instrument findings) of every blaze I detected.

Most days, though, it was the routine that occupied me. Up at seven or so every day, a pot of coffee brought to a boil over a handful of burning twigs, I'd go out in the alpine yard with a cup of coffee hooked in my thumb and leisurely make my wind speed and wind direction and temperature and moisture readings. Then, after chopping wood, I'd use the two-way radio and report to the relay station on Sourdough. At 10 A.M. I usually got hungry for breakfast, and I'd make delicious pancakes, eating them at my little table that was decorated with bouquets of mountain lupine and sprigs of fir.

Early in the afternoon was the usual time for my kick of the day, instant chocolate pudding with hot coffee. Around two or three, I'd lie on my back on the meadowside and watch the clouds float by, or pick blueberries and eat them right there. I had tuned the radio loud enough to hear any calls for Desolation.

Then at sunset I'd roust up my supper out of cans of yams and Spam and peas, or sometimes just pea soup with corn muffins baked on top of the wood stove in aluminum foil. Then I'd go out to that precipitous snow slope and shovel my two pails of snow for the water tub and gather an armful of fallen firewood from the hillside like the proverbial Old Woman of Japan. For the chipmunks and conies I put pans of leftovers under the shack; in the middle of the night I could hear them clanking around. The rat would scramble down from the attic and eat some too.

Sometimes I'd yell questions at the rocks and trees, and across gorges, or yodel, "What is the meaning of the void?" The answer was perfect silence, so I knew.

Before bedtime I'd read by kerosene lamp whatever books were in the shack. It's amazing how people in solitary hunger after books. After poring over every word of a medical tome, and the synopsized versions of Shakespeare's plays by Charles and Mary Lamb, I climbed up in the little attic and put together torn cowboy pocket books and magazines the mice had ravaged. I also played stud poker with three imaginary players.

Around bedtime I'd bring a cup of milk almost to a boil with a tablespoon of honey in it, and drink that for my lamby nightcap; then I'd curl up in my sleeping bag.

No man should go through life without once experiencing healthy, even bored solitude in the wilderness, finding himself depending solely on himself and thereby learning his true and hidden strength. Learning for instance, to eat when he's hungry and sleep when he's sleepy.

Also around bedtime was my singing time. I'd pace up and down the well-worn path in the dust of my rock singing all the show tunes I could remember, at the top of my voice, too, with nobody to hear except the deer and the bear.

In the red dusk, the mountains were symphonies in pink snow . . . Jack Mountain, Three Fools Peak, Freezeout Peak, Golden Horn, Mt. Terror, Mt. Fury, Mt. Despair, Crooked Thumb Peak, Mt. Challenger and the incomparable Mt. Baker bigger than the world in the distance . . . and my own little Jackass Ridge that completed the Ridge of Desolation. Pink snow and the clouds all distant and frilly like ancient remote cities of Buddhaland splendor, and the wind working incessantly—whish, whish—booming, at times rattling my shack.

For supper I made chop suey and baked some biscuits and put the leftovers in a pan for deer that came in the moonlit night and nibbled like big strange cows of peace— long-antlered buck and does and babies too—as I meditated in the alpine grass facing the magic moon-laned lake. And I could see firs reflected in the moonlit lake five thousand feet below, upside down, pointing to infinity.

And all the insects ceased in honor of the moon.

Sixty-three sunsets I saw revolve on that perpendicular hill . . . mad raging sunsets pouring in sea foams of cloud through unimaginable crags like the crags you grayly drew in pencil as a child, with every rose tint of hope beyond, making you feel just like them, brilliant and bleak beyond words.

Cold mornings with clouds billowing out of Lightning Gorge like smoke from a giant fire but the lake cerulean as ever.

August comes in with a blast that shakes your house and augurs little Augusticity . . . then that snowy-air and woodsmoke feeling . . . then the snow comes sweeping your way from Canada, and the wind rises and dark low clouds rush up as out of a forge. Suddenly a green-rose rainbow appears right on your ridge with steamy clouds all around and an orange sun turmoiling . . .

> What is a rainbow,
> Lord?—a hoop
> For the lowly

. . . and you go out and suddenly your shadow is ringed by the rainbow as you walk on the hilltop, a lovely-haloed mystery making you want to pray.

A blade of grass jiggling in the winds of infinity, anchored to a rock, and for your own poor gentle flesh no answer.

Your oil lamp burning in infinity.

One morning I found bear stool and signs of where the monster had taken a can of frozen milk and squeezed it in his paws and bit into it with one sharp tooth, trying to suck out the paste. In the foggy dawn I looked down the mysterious Ridge of Starvation with its fog-lost firs and its hills humping into invisibility, and the wind blowing the fog by like a faint blizzard, and I realized that somewhere in the fog stalked the bear.

And it seemed, as I sat there, that this was the Primordial Bear, and that he owned all the Northwest and all the snow and commanded all the mountains. He was King Bear, who could crush my head in his paws and crack my spine like a stick, and this was his house, his yard, his domain. Though I looked all day, he would not show himself in the mystery of those silent foggy slopes. He prowled at night among unknown lakes, and in the early morning the pearl-pure light that shadowed mountainsides of fir made him blink with respect. He had millenniums of prowling here behind him. He had seen the Indians and Redcoats come and go, and would see much more. He continuously heard the reassuring rapturous rush of silence, except when near creeks; he was aware of the light material the world is made of, yet he never discoursed, nor communicated by signs, nor wasted a breath complaining; he just nibbled and pawed, and lumbered along snags paying no attention to things inanimate or animate. His big mouth chew-chewed in the night, I could hear it across the mountain in the starlight. Soon he would come out of the fog, huge, and come and stare in my window with big burning eyes. He was Avalokitesvara the Bear, and his sign was the gray wind of autumn.

I was waiting for him. He never came.

Finally the autumn rains, all-night gales of soaking rain as I lie warm as toast in my sleeping bag and the mornings open cold wild fall days with high wind, racing fogs, racing clouds, sudden bright sun, pristine light on hill patches and my fire crackling as I exult and sing at the top of my voice. Outside my window a windswept chipmunk sits up straight on a rock, hands clasped as he nibbles an oat between his paws—the little nutty lord of all he surveys.

Thinking of the stars night after night I begin to realize "the stars are words" and all the innumerable worlds in the Milky Way are words, and so is this world too. And I realize that no matter where I am, whether in a little room full of thought, or in this endless universe of stars and mountains, it's all in my mind. There's no need for solitude. So love life for what it is, and form no preconceptions whatever in your mind.

When I came down in September a cool old golden look had come into the forest, auguring cold snaps and frost and the eventual howling blizzard that would cover my shack completely, unless those winds at the top of the world would keep her bald. As I reached the bend where the shack would disappear and I would plunge down to the lake to meet the boat that would take me out and home, I turned and blessed Desolation Peak and the little pagoda on top and thanked them for the shelter and the lesson I'd been taught.

Old Man Facing Death

by Oliver La Farge

A novelist portrays his father and defines a vital man's life from the perspective of his final days.

The relationship and common interests of two artists came late with my father and me. For us three brothers the early one, the constant running through our lives, was the outdoors, first the boats and the horses, then fishing, hunting, and on according as our various experiences matched his one way or another.

For me it begins with candlelight and a whisper. Long before dawn there would be the step on the stairs and the yellow clarity of the candle reaching through the doorway, spreading along the wall, growing stronger. Then his voice, conspiratorial, eager:

"Four o'clock, Inky. Get up."

He would leave the candle and slip downstairs, very quiet, a man to whom it came natural to tread lightly. I dressed in a hurry and followed him. A lamp and two alcohol flames burned in the dining room. In one copper kettle eggs were boiling, another, coffee, which otherwise I did not yet drink. There might be only me, or a brother or so as well. The eggs would be served soft-boiled. We hated soft-boiled eggs, but it never occurred to us to say a word. It was part of the ritual, along with the smell of the flames and hot copper and coffee, and my father constantly glancing out the window lest a gleam of white in the east proclaim us laggards.

All in whispers and soft movements. Guns ready. Rubber boots. The marsh and gun-oil smell of shooting jackets. Quietly down to the shore, the definite quality of escape, the canoe grating slightly on the beach, then the lap of water and the long paddle to the marshes.

You had the sense of being taken into a man's world; as Kipling said, of crossing to the men's side. A boy might be very much a pupil under instruction but at the same time my father let him feel that he was an equal partner in the joint enterprise of hunting. There was a thrilling promotion to equality in a private world. All hunting was illuminated by his artist's response to beauty and his trained perception, which he knew very well how to convey. When the duck came, when a trout rose to the fly, when there was a hen grouse with her chicks in the springtime or a butterfly hovering in sunlight, he could pull you alert and into perception with his quiet voice. There was an eternally fresh excitement in his speech and his eyes.

The voice was always quiet. He used the wild country as Indians do, in cooperation and communion with it, finding any form of noise a baneful disharmony. The impossible union of liquor and gunning which some men attempt, the loud talk sounding over waters, closing hearts and ears and eyes to the essence of hunting, were abomination to him. He called such sportsmen yahoos and taught us to hate the donkey-laugh in the woods as much as we do the mere killers. The Indians know a way of belonging to the manless country. Their ritual expresses the communion of love between a hunter and the game he seeks to kill. There is a way of being which fills with pleasure even the entirely luckless days when no game is seen or killed. These my father had.

Learning from him, we were always conscious of his reserves of experience. Canadian Indians accepted him as an equal canoeman. He was utterly at home in Arizona. He had sailed with our own Rhode Island fishermen long before a power-driven smack was dreamed of. The wild goose, the mountain goat, elk, salmon, moose, and caribou, snowshoes, pack-horses, tump-line and fishing-smack were his familiars. We became men and in one point or another achieved some single experience which we could match in talk with some part of his, but the older we grew and the more we learned, the deeper grew our respect.

This old man was practically indestructible. When he was seventy he decided I should have a real taste of Canadian-

style duck-hunting in a canoe. He put me in the bow
and took me upriver. With age he had shrunken very
slightly, a light, slender man with no great appearance of
strength about him. I knew he was good, but I did not
expect the force of his final twist of the paddle at each
stroke, the feel of the canoe leaping and turning under his
hand, all in nearly perfect silence. The loudest sound, I
think, was the fall of drops off his paddle as he reached
forward. Coming back downriver I took bow paddle. He was
nice about it, but the plain fact was that I was nowhere
near man enough to make an adequate mate for his stern
paddle.

It was about that time that the depression liquidated
his architectural practice. It took some persuading to talk
him out of starting over again from scratch. He had no
intention of becoming idle and quickly found new uses for
his skill and reputation.

It would not be quite true to say that he laughed off
his first heart attack, but it did not stop him from traveling
through Europe on a fellowship. The second one laid him
low. He had fished that spring, killed his duck in the fall,
then suddenly he was imprisoned in a small room with a
good view over the bay. After months he would be allowed
to walk about that floor, after yet longer he might be free
to go downstairs, carefully.

For more than a year we visited with him in the room.
Each of us received the same impression. Neither self-
deceived nor a coward, he was visibly making himself ready
for death. He let go, one by one, of minor interests and
particularly of those, such as improvements in the place,
which could be considered only in terms of years from
now. He kept up those which were rewarding in themselves and out of them made himself a lively life. He entertained himself with us.

I still do not know if there is a smell of death. There
was something in that room which had the emotional
effect of a smell, one felt the presence of the old skull and
bones. To him it must have been perched on the foot of
the bed. It might come in ten minutes and it might not
come for a year or more, there was no way of knowing.
It could come quietly, instantly, or it could strike as a sear-

ing, unbearable pain in the full fury of a heart attack.
None of this could be foreseen. It simply was always there,
waiting. And he knew it.

In its presence he sat up radiating his great personal
charm and his warmth at its most perfect. With me he
talked intimately about my writing, following my ideas and
endeavours with great interest, and endlessly we shared the
tribes we knew in common or matched this odd thing about
Guatemala with that of Canada. He was a very easy man
to talk to. He offered the wisdom of his many years and
at the same time he made himself contemporary.

When we came in from the river or the marshes we
went to his room and gave him a blow-by-blow account.
I started fishing at the big bend and put on a Queen of
the Waters and a Whirling Dun. That big bastard was feed-
ing under the log at the back of the bend, he rose to the
Queen a couple of times but wouldn't touch it. The marsh
marigolds were beautiful and there were some lady-slippers
out. At the log below the reach there was a good one feed-
ing. He took the Dun almost as it hit the water, here he
is. . . .

My father would listen, smiling, alert. At a lost fish or
a missed shot he would exclaim with the same disgust as
he had in the field, a success would give him the same
pleasure. When he detected a flaw in technique he would
advise as he always did.

Never, at any time, did he protest at being cooped up
in that room. None of us, nor my mother, heard him pity
himself for that, not even when we were on the marsh
with a fine sou'wester blowing. He would damn the cook
for a flavorless soup, row with my mother for ordering
food he didn't care for, in ten minutes he could cure
visitors he didn't like of coming to sit with him, when his
vitality was up he could raise particular hell over small
things. But he never complained about the big one, and
whatever fear sat on him, he never referred to it.

The fear was there along with the courage to handle it.
Death was in the room. You could not be there long and
not know that. Coming down for the weekend and entering
the room you were aware of it, it was oppressive and it
filled you with wonder at this man. Then he made you
forget it, and to the degree that you forgot it you recog-

nized it again after you had gone. The memory of that time is made up of his warmth, wide-ranging talk, laughter, his quick response, and that eternal presence. The two elements were in balance with each other, one could not separate them.

He had a shelf outside his window on which he put feed for the birds. Some of them were becoming very tame. There was a rat which came up the grapevine onto the porch roof at sundown and raided the feed. He had also killed a bird. My father wanted to get him. How about laying for him with the twenty-eight?

I took the little shotgun down from the shelf by the door. There were shells in his bureau. I mounted the gun and loaded it. Now we were back in our private world. It was dusk and the rat would come soon.

"Quiet, Inky. Sit here on the bed. He's smart, if you move he'll spot you."

The old voice, a whisper which you felt rather than heard and yet had the hunting timbre in it. The half smile and the lively eyes. We were hunting, sitting there in the growing darkness, he in the bed, I on it, waiting for a rat to show up. Hunting—my mind was divided, feeling his pleasure and thinking of the geese and duck coming in a howling snowstorm, of the big-horn and the moose and the mountain lion and the feats of skill and endurance. Hunting.

"Here he comes."

You didn't need to understand the words, you knew the all-but-inaudible, thrilling tone since you first crouched in a blind with him and the V of duck showed in the sky. Raising the gun and the click of the safety was too much, the rat fled back down the vine.

"Shah!" It was what he always said, and he made an adequate curse out of it. "They're so quick."

"We'll try again tomorrow evening."

I put the gun away and we went on with normal talk, but I was glad when I was called for supper. I needed time to cope with my sense of the pathetic.

His funeral was on the day before the season opened. That evening we spoke to my mother, and we all agreed that he would be most upset if we missed the opening day on his account. So the three of us went out and hunted for him. We felt tired, lax, and curiously peaceful. There was a great closeness to him in doing this, and none of us referred to him while we were out. We worked unusually carefully, and we had good luck. When my mother saw our bag, as many black duck as we had use for, she said:

"Oh, boys, your father would be so pleased."

In a sense I have hunted with him ever since and discussed the problems that arose with him. Often I talk to him in Spanish, a language he loved and which was one of our common interests. Then he is the man of the first thirty-five years of my life, the woodsman who could always walk me groggy. At other times it occasionally happens that I think about my own death, and pray that it will be sudden. And if it comes slowly I wonder and doubt if I could turn the old skeleton into a mere visitor sitting to one side while I entertained myself by fascinating my friends.

Portrait of Hemingway—
Preface, 1961

by Lillian Ross

*Upon Ernest Hemingway's death in 1961, a New Yorker
reporter, who wrote a controversial profile of him eleven
years earlier, reconsiders the famous American as a
writer, as a reader and as a man.*

I first met Ernest Hemingway on the day before
Christmas in 1947, in Ketchum, Idaho. I was on my way
back to New York from Mexico, where I had gone to see
Sidney Franklin, the American bullfighter from Brooklyn,
about whom I was trying to write my first Profile for
The New Yorker. Hemingway had known Franklin as a
bullfighter in Spain in the late twenties and early thirties.
I had gone to some *corridas* in Mexico with Franklin, and
had been appalled and scared to death when I got my first
look at what goes on in a bull ring. Although I appreciated
the matador's cape work with the bulls, and the colorful,
ceremonial atmosphere, I wasn't fond of bullfighting as
such. I guess what interested me was just how Franklin, son
of a hardworking policeman in Flatbush, had become a
bullfighter. When Franklin told me that Hemingway was
the first American who had ever spoken to him intelli-
gently about bullfighting, I telephoned Hemingway in Ketchum. Hemingway liked spending vacations there, skiing
and hunting, away from his home in San Francisco de
Paula, near Havana, Cuba, and later on he bought a house
in Ketchum. When I called, Hemingway was staying in a
tourist cabin with his wife, Mary, his sons—John, Pat-
rick, and Gregory—and some fishing friends from Cuba,
and he hospitably invited me to drop in and see him on
my way back East.

The first time I saw Hemingway was about seven o'clock
in the morning, in front of his tourist cabin, shortly after

my train got in. He was standing on hard-packed snow, in dry cold of ten degrees below zero, wearing bedroom slippers, no socks, Western trousers with an Indian belt that had a silver buckle, and a lightweight Western-style sports shirt open at the collar and with button-down pockets. He had a graying mustache but had not yet started to wear the patriarchal-looking beard that was eventually to give him an air of saintliness and innocence—an air that somehow or other never seemed to be at odds with his ruggedness. That morning, he looked rugged and burly and eager and friendly and kind. I was wearing a heavy coat, but I was absolutely freezing in the cold. However, Hemingway, when I asked him, said he wasn't a bit cold. He seemed to have tremendous built-in warmth. I spent a wonderful day of talk and Christmas shopping with the Hemingways and their friends. Mary Hemingway, like her husband, was warm and gracious and knowledgeable, as well as capable of brilliantly filling the difficult role of famous writer's wife. She enjoyed the same things he did, and seemed to me to be the perfect partner for him.

Shortly after my Ketchum visit, Hemingway wrote to me from Cuba that he thought I was the person least suited in the world to do an article on bullfighting. Nevertheless, I went ahead, and eventually did finish the Profile of Franklin. After the magazine's editors had accepted it, I sent Hemingway some queries about it, and he replied most helpfully in a letter winding up with the statement that he looked forward with horror to reading it. In the meantime, though, *The New Yorker* published a couple of shorter pieces of mine, and Hemingway and his wife, both regular readers of the magazine (he once wrote me that my mob was his mob, too), seemed to like them. When the Franklin Profile was published, I had a letter from Hemingway, scrawled in pencil, from Villa Aprile, Cortina d'Ampezzo, Italy, in which he said that what he called the Sidney pieces were fine. In his crowded life, he did his best to remember exactly what he had said to you before, and he made a point, generously, of correcting himself when he felt that it was necessary. His compliments were straight and honest, and they were designed to make people feel good. He might call you reliable and compare you to Joe Page and Hugh Casey, and you wouldn't have to be an archivist of baseball to realize you were being praised. The way he wrote in his letters, the way he talked, in itself made me feel good—it was so fresh and wonderful. He was generous in his conversation. He didn't hoard his ideas or his thoughts or his humor or his opinions. He was so inventive that he probably had the feeling there was plenty more where that came from. But whatever his feeling might have been, he would have talked as he did out of sheer generosity. He offered so much in what he said, and always with fun and with sharp understanding and compassion and sensitivity. When he talked, he was free. The sound and the content were marvellously alive.

In the spring of 1950, I wrote a Profile of Hemingway for *The New Yorker*. It was a sympathetic piece, covering two days Hemingway spent in New York, in which I tried to describe as precisely as possible how Hemingway, who had the nerve to be like nobody else on earth, looked and sounded when he was in action, talking, between work periods—to give a picture of the man as he was, in his uniqueness and with his vitality and his enormous spirit of fun intact. Before it was published, I sent a galley proof of it to the Hemingways, and they returned it marked with corrections. In an accompanying letter, Hemingway said that he had found the Profile funny and good, and that he had suggested only one deletion. Then a strange and mysterious thing happened. Nothing like it had ever happened before in my writing experience, or has happened since. To the complete surprise of Hemingway and the editors of *The New Yorker* and myself, it turned out, when the Profile appeared, that what I had written was extremely controversial. Most readers took the piece for just what it was, and I trust that they enjoyed it in an uncomplicated fashion. However, a certain number of readers reacted violently, and in a very complicated fashion. Among these were people who objected strongly to Hemingway's personality, assumed I did the same, and admired the piece for the wrong reasons; that is, they thought that in describing that personality accurately I was ridiculing or attacking it. Other people simply didn't like the way Hemingway talked (they even objected to the playful way he sometimes dropped his articles and spoke a kind of joke Indian language); they didn't like his freedom; they didn't like

his not taking himself seriously; they didn't like his wast-
ing his time on going to boxing matches, going to the zoo,
talking to friends, going fishing, enjoying people, celebrat-
ing his approach to the finish of a book by splurging on
caviar and champagne; they didn't like this and they didn't
like that. In fact, they didn't like Hemingway to be Hemingway. They wanted him to be somebody else—probably
themselves. So they came to the conclusion that either
Hemingway had not been portrayed as he was or, if he
was that way, I shouldn't have written about him at all.
Either they had dreary, small-minded preconceptions about
how a great writer should behave and preferred their preconceptions to the facts or they attributed to me their own
pious disapproval of Hemingway and then berated me for
it. Some of the more devastation-minded among them called
the Profile "devastating." When Hemingway heard about
all this, he wrote to reassure me. On June 16, 1950, he
wrote that I shouldn't worry about the piece and that it
was just that people got things all mixed up. A number of
times he wrote about the attitude of people he called the
devastate people. Some people, he said, couldn't understand his enjoying himself and his not being really spooky;
they couldn't understand his being a serious writer without being pompous.

Death puts certain things in perspective. No doubt if
some of the people who misunderstood the Profile were
to read it now, they would see it for what it is. When I
wrote the Profile, I attempted to set down only what I
had seen and heard, and not to comment on the facts or
express any opinions or pass any judgments. However, I
believe that today—with the advantage gained by distance
—almost any reader would see that, although I did not reveal my viewpoint directly, implicit in my choice and
arrangement of detail, and in the total atmosphere created,
was my feeling of affection and admiration. I liked Hemingway exactly as he was, and I'm content if my Profile
caught him exactly as he was during those two days in
New York.

While I'm at it, as somebody who has never been concerned with "rating" Hemingway's works but has simply
been grateful for whatever joy his writing has offered, I
might as well throw in a word about those critics who

took an injured, censorious tone when discussing the life that Hemingway led in later years and what they considered a decline in his work. They sometimes sounded as if they thought that Hemingway made a point of letting them, specifically, down, in order to disport himself as a public figure, whereas, as I saw it, he was heroically and uncorruptedly and uncompromisingly occupied day after day with writing as hard as *he could* and as well as *he could* until the day he died. And when he was unable to write or was between books, he still did what *he could,* which was to live life to the full and then, with that limitless generosity of his, make his private experience public, so that everybody else could also have a wonderful time.

Hemingway was generous in so many different ways. In his letters and in his conversations with friends, Hemingway gave away the very substance out of which another man might have created an entire body of work. The style of Hemingway's letters was a separate style, free and loose and (since he knew that time was short) full of his own shorthand—much freer, as one might expect, than his formal writing. He was a tireless correspondent. I went out to Hollywood for a year and a half after the Profile appeared, to write a series of articles about the making of a movie, and I received scores of letters from Hemingway out there, giving me his views on movies and movie-making and life on the Coast, and also keeping me informed, and entertained, with accounts of his fishing and other adventures in Cuba. When he went to Africa to hunt in 1953, he wrote about the wonders of life there. Africa, he told me, was in many ways the best life of all, and I ought to come there and try it. He usually ended his letters by asking you to write soon. He didn't like to stop writing letters, he once told me, because then he wouldn't receive any, and that would make it lonely. Occasionally, Mary would write a letter, and it would have Hemingway's own kind of enthusiasm and humor. She would write from Kenya that it was the greatest place in the world for waking up in the morning, and that you had to encounter a live, two-ton rhinoceros before dawn, on your way to wash your face, to appreciate what living could be. A lot of other people the Hemingways knew—people who knew them better than I did—probably also got invitations to come there and try it. The Hemingways were always hospitable and friendly. They were always inviting you to visit them in Kenya or in Paris or at their farm in Cuba. I'm sorry that I was never able to do it.

Nobody could fool Hemingway about writing or about writers. He knew both, and he knew them deeply. He knew when a writer was worthless or a fraud, no matter how great the writer's reputation or his sales or his advances from movie companies. About himself he wrote, on August 8, 1950, that all his life he had tried to learn to write better and to know and understand. People, he said, imitated his defects, stole his cadences and rhythms, and called the result the Hemingway school of writing, and nobody wished him well. Then he had an afterthought, and wrote that that was wrong, that a lot of people wished him well but just didn't, he guessed, tell him about it. Writing and literature he took seriously. And whatever he was asked for he always tried to give. He was quick to respond to younger writers. Once, I asked him to give me a list of reading that he would recommend. He composed the following list:

"Boule de Suif" and "La Maison Tellier"—de Maupassant
  The Red and the Black—Stendhal
  Les Fleurs du Mal—Baudelaire
  Madame Bovary—Flaubert
  Remembrance of Things Past—Proust
  Buddenbrooks—Mann
  Taras Bulba—Gogol
  The Brothers Karamazov—Dostoevski
  Anna Karenina and *War and Peace*—Tolstoy
  Huckleberry Finn—Twain
  Moby Dick—Melville
  The Scarlet Letter—Hawthorne
  The Red Badge of Courage—Crane
  Madame de Mauves—James

Whatever you brought up with Hemingway, he always tried—or so I found—to give you a response that would be helpful. At one point, after finishing a long piece of work, I told him that I wanted to write shorter and easier pieces from then on. His answer was that I would have to write harder ones and better ones until I died. Only, don't die, he added, explaining that that was the only thing he knew that was really worthless. He was helpful with minor matters, too. When I was in California, trying to learn to ride a horse, Hemingway advised me not to ride any big or fat horses but to get the smallest, smartest, and least mean horse there was. About Hollywood his advice was succinct. He told me not to stay too long.

Hemingway has been called romantic, as distinguished from realistic, about life, especially by some of the heavy thinkers. It always seemed to me that Hemingway was a sound observer and understander of the realities. Once, I passed along some pleasant remarks I had heard about his son John, and Hemingway wrote back that he loved his son very much and then went on to say that in his lifetime he had also loved three continents, several airplanes and ships, the oceans, his sisters, his wives, life and death, morning, noon, evening, and night, honor, bed, boxing, swimming, baseball, shooting, fishing, and reading and writing and all good pictures.

Not long before he died, when he was at the Mayo Clinic, in Rochester, Minnesota, Hemingway wrote to me that he had his blood-pressure "nonsense" licked again but that he was behind in his work, and that he and Mary were taking off soon for some place where people would leave them alone and "let me write."

Real Women

by Robert Graves

A mythologist-poet examines the various historical concepts of the place of women and presents his own definition of her twentieth-century role.

The most important historical study of all, utterly dwarfing all economic and political ones, is for me the changing relationship between men and women down the centuries—from prehistoric times to the present moral chaos in which both sexes have become equally confused about their roles. But I am a poet by calling, and have lived outside ordinary civilization for so many years that anything I write about real women must read oddly. Except perhaps to real women themselves, and the occasional man whom some accident of birth or experience tempts to agree with me.

A real woman, by my definition, neither despises nor worships men, but is proud not to have been born a man, does everything she can to avoid thinking of acting like one, knows the full extent of her powers, and feels free to reject all arbitrary man-made obligations. She is her own oracle of right and wrong, firmly believing in her five sound senses and the intuitive sixth. Once a real woman has been warned by her nose that those apples are tasteless, or assured by her fingertips that this material is shoddy, no salesman in the world can persuade her to the contrary. Nor, once she has met some personage in private, and summed him up with a single keen glance as weak, vain or crooked, will his mounting public reputation convince her otherwise. She takes pleasure in the company of simple, happy, undemanding women; but seldom or never finds a friend worthy of her full confidence. Since she never settles for the second best in love, what most troubles her is the rareness of real men. Wherever she goes, her singularity will arouse strong feelings: adulation, jealousy, resentment, but never pity for her loneliness. Real women are royal women; the words once had the same meaning. Democracy has no welcome for queens.

It would be wrong to identify the real woman with the typical wild one who, after a difficult childhood, has left home early to live by her wits at the expense of men. The wild woman is incapable either of friendship for other women, whom she cannot fail to regard as rivals, or of love for a man, her declared enemy. But at least she keeps her eyes open and ridicules the view that women must enthusiastically accept this glorious modern world of plenty bestowed on them by their hardworking menfolk, and that they enjoy being passionately swept off their feet and afterward treated with amused indulgence. There was never, of course, any truth in the comic-strip legend of a primitive he-man who would grab his woman by the hair, threaten her with a knobbed club if she refused his advances, and haul her off panting ecstatically to his cave. In ancient Majorca, the island which I have made my home for more than thirty years, the woman, not the man, owned their cave; and, according to the Roman historian Strabo, if he took things too much for granted, she would merely say, "Begone, and take your possessions with you," and out he had to go—the children were hers in any case.

To reach some understanding of real women, one must think back to a primitive age, when men invariably treated women as the holier sex, since they alone perpetuated the race. Women were the sole agriculturists, guardians of springs, fruit trees, and the sacred hearth fire, and lived unaffected by any notions of progress. Tribal queens never thought in terms of historical time, but only of seasons; judged each case on its own merits, not by a legal code, as real women still do; and showed little regard for trade or mechanical invention. Chance discoveries or new techniques in arts and crafts were welcome, so long as these neither upset tribal economy nor enhanced the importance of individuals. It was the queen's task to restrain men from letting their ambition or intellectual curiosity override practical common sense, as it is still the woman's task to ask her husband: "Must you kill yourself making money? Haven't we enough for the next five years at least, even if you stopped working altogether? Surely you don't enjoy your martyrdom?" But even if he cared to listen, social pressures compel him to provide for his family until he drops dead.

History begins with the emergence of men from female rule. They had at last discovered that a woman cannot conceive without male assistance—and brooded over the implications of this surprising fact. After long whispered conferences it was agreed that men ought to claim their freedom. They asked, "Why should descent be reckoned in the female line, not the male? Why should a man when he marries go to the woman's home, not contrariwise? Why should a woman, not a man, sow the seed corn? Why should women control the tribe? Surely men are the true creators, sowers of seed, and therefore the holier sex, as well as being physically stronger?" Thus the male habit of reasoning from irrelevant facts, rather than relying on woman's practical wisdom, began the war between the sexes that has been raging ever since.

Men gradually usurped women's prerogatives in farming, magic, handicrafts, war—the Amazons are no mere figment—and government. The story is epitomized in a classical Greek myth: how the goddess Hera pitied a poor, bedraggled cuckoo and warmed him at her breast. This cuckoo was her brother Zeus in disguise, who ravished and humiliated her by seizing throne and scepter. Later, when Hera and her kinsfolk rebelled against Zeus, he hung her from the vault of heaven, with an anvil tied to each foot. . . .

Men consolidated their victory. They reckoned descent in the male line, brought wives to their own homes, invented historical annals, legal codes, weights and measures, standing armies, engineering, logic and philosophy. On the excuse of protecting the weaker sex, they placed woman under male tutelage: henceforward she must serve her father's or husband's domestic needs as though not only spiritually but mentally inferior to him.

Greek myths record an occasional dramatic protest against this state of affairs: how the fifty Danaides stabbed their husbands, the sons of Aegyptus, on their common wedding night, and were punished in hell for this crime;

how the Lemnian women murdered theirs for importing concubines from Thrace; how Amazons attacked Athens. . . . Yet, as a rule, the sex war has been fought sporadically in the home between father and daughter, husband and wife, mother-in-law and son-in-law. Only isolated regions, such as Galicia, Majorca and Pictish Scotland, kept their matriarchal traditions.

It seems puzzling that the real women of those days let all this happen to them. The sole reason I can suggest is that they thought far ahead. Since man had a certain undeveloped intellectual capacity, of which it would have been wrong to deny him full use, the real women sat back patiently, prepared to give him a free hand for some hundreds or thousands of years. Only a long series of disastrous experiments could make him realize the error of his headstrong ways. Eventually he must return to them in willing and chastened dependence.

Priests of the new male gods even modified the ancient myth of a sole goddess who had created the world, giving her a male assistant; and in Genesis—a comparatively late book—Jehovah creates the world entirely by Himself; and models Eve, the first woman, from man's rib! It is added that this woman's disobedience to God caused man to stumble and sin. In fact, the story is based on a Hebrew pun: the same word means both "rib" and "make to stumble." According to Hesiod's contemporary Greek myth, an inquisitive woman named Pandora opened a divine jar entrusted to her and let loose on mankind all the evils that now plague us. Yet "Eve" was originally a title of the sole creatrix; as was also "Pandora."

Financial pressures of men's own making brought about the recent so-called emancipation of women. Grown daughters could no longer stay idling at home, a burden to their parents and to themselves until married off. Industry was booming and, with appropriate moral safeguards, they might fill the widening gaps in manpower. Women, who can now earn and keep their own money, even when wives, and have been granted the franchise—"franchise" originally meant "freedom from being a serf"—need show men no gratitude for this liberality. Their freedom is still limited. They remain citizens of the second degree, auxiliary male personnel barred from all the highest offices; and would never have got where they are so quickly had it not been for two world wars and such loveless male inventions as machine guns, submarines, bombing planes and universal conscription.

Strangely enough, it is easier to be a real woman in backwaters of Christianity or Islam or Hinduism, where codes of behavior have not changed for centuries, than in urbanized Europe or America. There she knows what part she must play, and can guard her inborn dignity. Although the husband, as head of the family, makes all decisions, he will never dare overrule even her unspoken protests. Among Majorcan peasants who live beyond the tourist range, no man would ever think of buying or selling so much as a hen without his wife's approval. She is always referred to as *la madonna,* the titular guardian of the home.

What is home? In ancient days it meant a clan settlement, a camp or kraal, ruled by elders, where men had comrades and women their gossips, and children ran about in packs; and where a happy man-woman relationship could exist in some small corner away from the communal bustle.

Among us Westerners, because of man's jealous insistence on marital privacy, *home* has shrunk from settlement to farmhouse, thence to the cottage, thence to the ten-roomed apartment, thence to three rooms and a kitchenette with the usual labor-saving devices, in a huge residential block full of utter strangers. The housewife has her washing machine, telephone, television, refrigerator, electric cookstove, car and door keys, to pay for which a husband must be out working all week. She cannot regret (because she never knew) the easy companionship of her great-grandmother's day: quilting bees and husking bees, taking the cousins to do a week's washing down at the creek, lending a hand with the shearing and harvest, making jams and pickles, getting up round dances, singing and playing practical jokes. But no real woman can ever accept the present situation.

Man's logic has defeated itself. Boredom often drives the married woman back to a job as soon as she can leave her children at a nursery school; or to infidelity; or to an analyst. Home is home for only two days of the week. Which is why some paternally minded industrialists take advice from professors of sociology and plant their employees all together in a wholesome suburban neighborhood, where the company's standards of taste and respectability must rule their lives. Husband obeys boss; wife obeys husband, and preserves amicable relations with her fellow company wives or else. . . . Spouses are thus shackled by a well-paid job to which the husband need no longer commute, by house, garden and swimming pool, by children, by hope of advancement and the prospect of a pension. Any sign of noncompliance is scored against both. No real woman can ever accept this situation either.

Attempts to liven things up socially are all too often masked under the dubious name of charity. It is characteristic of a real woman never to support public charities— on the ground that she neither knows the person to whom her money goes nor has any assurance that it will be properly distributed. She gives only to those whose needs are familiar to her, and then from friendship, not pity. She will not be found at bridge clubs or at cocktail parties. Bridge, which is, after all, a money contest between individual players, cannot be a substitute for the good humor of a communal washday; nor can a cocktail party for the intimate gossip of a quilting bee.

Wild women take advantage of this artificial state of affairs by exploiting the dormant dissatisfactions of husbands. One of them told me the other day, "Yes, you may call me a mean, greedy, undependable, lazy, treacherous, spendthrift bitch. That's true enough a good part of the time; but it isn't the whole story. In fact, I've given myself to myself, and to no one else. My beauty is my own, and I take good care of it. If I choose a lover, I grant the lucky fellow no right over me; and if he has sense, he won't claim any. As for breaking up a home, nobody can do that unless it's already cracked!"

A real woman likes beautiful things of her own choosing. She prefers a handleless cup, a backless chair, a mattress on the floor and a packing case for the table to good taste conferred on her wholesale by interior decorators. There is an eighteenth-century English song, "Sally in Our Alley":

Her father, he sells cabbage nets
And through the streets doth cry 'em.
Her mother, she sells laces long
To such as care to buy 'em—
Who'd think such rascals could beget
So sweet a girl as Sally?
She is the darling of my heart
And lives in our alley . . .

The lover was a square: an honest, idealistic London apprentice, intent on becoming a journeyman, a master craftsman and eventually a rich merchant—perhaps even Lord Mayor:

When Eastertide comes round again
Oh, then I'll have some money—
I'll save it up, and box and all
I'll give it to my honey . . .
And then my seven years' time is o'er
Oh, then I'll marry Sally,
Ay, then we'll wed, and then we'll bed—
But not in our alley!

The broken-down, foul-smelling alley was a settlement, a home, the denizens of which were bound together by common poverty, shiftlessness, pugnacity, humor and a hatred of landlords and police. Yet no well-planned housing estate can ever compete with its spirit, which a Sally was always found to keep alive. From 1940 to '43 the German blitz leveled what remained of these alleys, and their sites are now occupied by large all-glass office blocks. The last of the Sallies found herself in a suburban life-box—one of hundreds built to the same design and set down in parallel rows—longing for a return to poverty, vice, dirt and even flying bombs.

Marriage, like money, is still with us; and, like money, progressively devalued. The ties between these two male inventions get closer and closer. Originally marriage meant the sale of a woman by one man to another; now most women sell themselves though they have no intention of delivering the goods listed in the bill of sale. Not only is the wife, on an average, five years younger than her husband, but she lives statistically longer. So money power passes progressively into the hands of women. Also, divorce legislation (forced on guilt-ridden legislators by nagging spouses) grossly favors the wife. A youthful rival figures in most divorce suits, and though she and the wife seldom act collusively, they share an old-fashioned insistence on the honorable state of marriage, which enriches both. Wild women will commit matrimony when things go hard for them, without the least thought of keeping their obligations. The entranced husbands never know what has hit them, nor do they profit by the experience.

The United States, though often described as a matriarchy in all but name, remains patriarchal. Matriarchy, to be effective, needs real women. When women organize themselves intellectually on masculine lines, they merely stimulate the feminization of men, who, for terror of husband-hunting viragoes, are apt to seek refuge in the cul-de-sac of homosexuality.

Though men are more conventional than women and fear to infringe the Mosaic law (Deuteronomy XXII.5) which forbids their wearing of women's clothes, women have no scruples about flouting the companion law: "The woman shall not wear that which pertaineth unto a man . . . for all that do so are abomination unto the Lord. . . ." Even matrons now unblushingly wear blue jeans zipped in front.

The pseudopatriarchal trend encourages women to respect legality, which they had hitherto found distasteful. A real woman, giving evidence in a court of law, scorns factual truth. Should her sense of equity run counter to the formal demands of justice, she will perjure herself in replies of cool and convincing honesty. When obliged to exercise a vote, she scorns the male axiom that the majority is always right.

A few real women survive in the old royal sense among West African queens, who rule with a silver knot-of-wisdom scepter and claim the moon goddess Ngame as their remote ancestress. A "knot of wisdom"—known in English as the "true lover's knot"—is the sort that tightens more securely the harder you tug at either end. Symbolically it means, "My command can never be disobeyed!"

In civilized society royal women have neither thrones

nor territorial queendoms, but the moon inspires them still, and they can wield formidable powers in times of emergency. Yet, since they avoid becoming public figures—the personality cult is another male invention—their names pass into history far more seldom than those of notorious wild women. A remarkable exception was Elizabeth I of England, whom her poets addressed as Cynthia—"The Moon"—and whose cynical disparagement of herself as "but a weak woman" concealed an unshaken faith in her royal wisdom. Elizabeth ruled through awe and love, was on playful terms with her ladies-in-waiting, inspired her male subjects to feats of heroism and flights of poetry never known before or since among the English, always said "No" to a doubtful petition and then slept on it.

A real woman's main concern is her beauty, which she cultivates for her own pleasure—not to ensnare men. Though she despises fashion as a male financial business, she will not make herself conspicuous by a defiance of conventions. The materials, colors and cut of her clothes, her hair style and her jewels are all chosen to match a sense of personal uniqueness. She can dress in advance of fashion, yet seem to lead it; and to any irregular features she may have, she lends a lovely ugliness denied to common beauty queens. Perfect detachment from the artificial or secondhand keeps her face unclouded. She has no small talk on current topics, and will suddenly vanish from a party, however grand, as soon as it grows boring.

If she plays games, it will be for fun, not competition; and if up against a win-at-all-costs opponent in tennis or golf, she will take care to lose handsomely—as one who competes only against herself. If she drinks, it will because she likes the taste; and if she smokes, it will be for the same reason, not to steady her nerve.

She misses real men—men who would recognize her potentiality and agree that our world, despite its appearance of rational organization, is a wholly haphazard one, clanking on noisily to its fate along a random course once defined as "progress." And that a calamitous collapse must come before a new start can be made—from the point where the sex war was first declared and woman's conservative instinct as the guiding force of humankind repudiated. Because womanhood remains incomplete without a child, most real women marry—preferring simple, affectionate husbands who cannot understand them. This is not a renunciation of real love, since they agree with the thirteenth-century Countess of Narbonne: "Conjugal affection has absolutely nothing in common with love. We say 'absolutely,' and with all consideration, that love cannot exist between husband and wife."

Man's biological function is to do; woman's is to be. This difference is not a contrast of mere activity with mere passivity. "To be" is indeed a full-time occupation. A real woman has no leisure in the modern economic sense—leisure as a consumer's relaxed insistence on commercial entertainment—but is always thinking, taking stock of herself, setting a stage on which actors can perform. If she paints or writes, this will be for her own private amusement, not to satisfy ambition; and if forced to earn her livelihood in this way, she repudiates the public personage forced on her by dealers and critics.

A real woman is content to dress with a difference, to make her home unmistakably her own, to illuminate any company she enters, to cook by instinct, not by the cookbook. This is her evidence of being, the proof of which lies in her sense of certitude. She is no feminist; feminism, like all "isms," implies an intellectual approach to a subject; and reality can be understood only by transcending the intellect.

Mental institutions on both sides of the Atlantic house hundreds of young, beautiful, silently brooding girls, victims of the sex war—defeated before they could come to terms with life. Their tragedy has been brilliantly described in *The Ha-Ha,* a novel by Jennifer Dawson, whose heroine is almost a real woman, because: "she never just plays a game with herself or other people, and refuses to learn the rules of society—meaning the worthy, useful, ordinary women who are so busy finding husbands and houses and good income brackets that they just haven't time to be conscious of themselves, and who see the world as an inventory, a container of so many things, and other people as so many tin-openers to undo it for them."

The friendly and intelligent staff of the mental institution cannot persuade her that she should realign herself with the orderly outside male world. Being not quite real enough to escape defeat by pretending conformity, she loses all pride in her appearance, ceases to concentrate on any self-imposed task; and when at last she desperately breaks out, the police, we know, cannot fail to fetch her back for sedation and still closer surveillance.

A real woman somehow avoids suicide, or virtual suicide, or the mental institution; but is always painfully aware of having been born out of her true epoch; considered as either the past, or as the long-distant future. A sense of humor saves her from defeat. "This is not worthy of me," she will remind herself ten times a day, "but to preserve my inner self I must once more act an alien part."

None of her women neighbors, idly content with money and what it will buy, feel any need for drastic change in the man-woman relationship; she treats them politely, and has patience. If she ever comes across a real man, the thin thread of human hope—that eventually the world will make practical sense again—cannot yet have snapped.

*Searching for
Meaning
in a Complex Society*

What I Believe

by E. M. Forster

A novelist-critic analyzes contemporary society's faith in great causes and rejects them in favor of a personal belief in himself and in any man who can live as if there were no death.

I do not believe in belief. But this is an age of faith, where one is surrounded by so many militant creeds that, in self-defense, one has to formulate a creed of one's own. Tolerance, good temper, and sympathy are no longer enough in a world which is rent by religious and racial persecution, in a world where ignorance rules, and science, who ought to have ruled, plays the subservient pimp. Tolerance, good temper, and sympathy—well, they are what matter really, and if the human race is not to collapse they must come to the front before long. But for the moment they don't seem enough, their action is no stronger than a flower, battered beneath a military jack boot. They want stiffening, even if the process coarsens them. Faith, to my mind, is a stiffening process, a sort of mental starch, which ought to be applied as sparingly as possible. I dislike the stuff. I do not believe in it, for its own sake, at all. Herein I probably differ from most of the contributors to this volume, who believe in belief, and are only sorry they can't swallow even more than they do. My lawgivers are Erasmus and Montaigne, not Moses and St. Paul. My temple stands not upon Mount Moriah but in the Elysian Field where even the immoral are admitted. My motto is "Lord, I disbelieve—help thou my unbelief."

I have, however, to live in an age of Faith—the sort of thing I used to hear praised and recommended when I was a boy. It is damned unpleasant, really. It is bloody in every sense of the word. And I have to keep my end up in it. Where do I start?

With personal relationships. Here is something comparatively solid in a world full of violence and cruelty. Not absolutely solid, for psychology has split and shattered the idea of a "person," and has shown that there is something incalculable in each of us, which may at any moment rise to the surface and destroy our normal balance. We don't know what we're like. We can't know what other people are like. How then can we put any trust in personal relationships, or cling to them in the gathering political storm? In theory we can't. But in practice we can and do. Though A isn't unchangeably A or B unchangeably B, there can still be love and loyalty between the two. For the purpose of living one has to assume that the personality is solid, and the "self" is an entity, and to ignore all contrary evidence. And since to ignore evidence is one of the characteristics of faith, I certainly can proclaim that I believe in personal relationships.

Starting from them, I get a little order into the contemporary chaos. One must be fond of people and trust them if one isn't to make a mess of life, and it is therefore essential that they shouldn't let one down. They often do. The moral of which is that I must myself be as reliable as possible, and this I try to be. But reliability isn't a matter of contract—that is the main difference between the world of personal relationships and the world of business relationships. It is a matter for the heart, which signs no documents. In other words, reliability is impossible unless there is a natural warmth. Most men possess this warmth, though they often have bad luck and get chilled. Most of them, even when they are politicians, *want* to keep faith. And one can, at all events, show one's own little light here, one's own poor little trembling flame, with the knowledge that it's not the only light that is shining in the darkness, and not the only one which the darkness doesn't comprehend. Personal relations are despised today. They are regarded as bourgeois luxuries, as products of a time of fair weather which has now passed, and we are urged to get rid of them, and to dedicate ourselves to some movement or cause instead. I hate the idea of dying for a cause, and if I had to choose between betraying my country and betraying my friend, I hope I should have the guts to betray my country. Such a choice may scandalize the modern reader, and he may stretch out his patriotic hand to the telephone at once, and ring up the police. It wouldn't have shocked Dante, though. Dante places Brutus and Cassius in the lowest circle of Hell because they had chosen to betray their friend Julius Caesar rather than their country Rome. Probably one won't be asked to make such an agonizing choice. Still there lies at the back of every creed something terrible and hard for which the worshiper may one day be required to suffer, and there is even a terror and a hardness in this creed of personal relationships, urbane and mild though it sounds. Love and loyalty to an individual can run counter to the claims of the state. When they do—down with the state, say I, which means that the state will down me.

This brings me along to democracy, "even Love, the Beloved Republic, which feeds upon Freedom and lives." Democracy isn't a beloved republic really, and never will be. But it is less hateful than other contemporary forms of government, and to that extent it deserves our support. It does start from the assumption that the individual is important, and that all types are needed to make a civilization. It doesn't divide its citizens into the bossers and the bossed, as an efficiency regime tends to do. The people I admire most are those who are sensitive and want to create something or discover something, and don't see life in terms of power, and such people get more of a chance under democracy than elsewhere. They found religions, great or small, or they produce literature and art, or they do disinterested scientific research, or they may be what is called "ordinary people," who are creative in their private lives, bring up their children decently, for instance, or help their neighbors. All these people need to express themselves, they can't do so unless society allows them liberty to do so, and the society which allows them most liberty is a democracy.

Democracy has another merit. It allows criticism, and if there isn't public criticism there are bound to be hushed up scandals. That is why I believe in the press, despite all its lies and vulgarity, and why I believe in Parliament. The British Parliament is often sneered at because it's a talking shop. Well, I believe in it because it is a talking shop. I believe in the private member who makes himself a nuisance. He gets snubbed and is told that he is cranky or ill-informed, but he exposes abuses which would otherwise never have been mentioned, and very often an abuse gets put right just by being mentioned. Occasionally, too, in my country, a well-meaning public official loses his head in the cause of efficiency, and thinks himself God Almighty. Such officials are particularly frequent in the Home Office. Well, there will be questions about them in Parliament sooner or later, and then they'll have to mend their steps. Whether Parliament is either a representative body or an efficient one is very doubtful, but I value it because it criticizes and talks, and because its chatter gets widely reported.

So two cheers for democracy: one because it admits variety and two because it permits criticism. Two cheers are quite enough: there is no occasion to give three. Only Love, the Beloved Republic deserves that.

What about force, though? While we are trying to be sensitive and advanced and affectionate and tolerant, an unpleasant question pops up: Doesn't all society rest upon force? If a government can't count upon the police and the army, how can it hope to rule? And if an individual gets knocked on the head or sent to a labor camp, of what significance are his opinions?

This dilemma doesn't worry me as much as it does some. I realize that all society rests upon force. But all the great creative actions, all the decent human relations, occur during the intervals when force has not managed to come to the front. These intervals are what matter. I want them to be as frequent and as lengthy as possible and I call them "civilization." Some people idealize force and pull it into the foreground and worship it, instead of keeping it in the background as long as possible. I think they make a mistake, and I think that their opposites, the mystics, err even more when they declare that force doesn't exist. I believe that it does exist, and that one of our jobs is to prevent it from getting out of its box. It gets out sooner or later, and then it destroys us and all the lovely things which we have made. But it isn't out all the time, for the fortunate reason that the strong are so stupid. Consider their conduct for a moment in the Nibelung's *Ring*. The giants there have the guns, or in other words the gold; but they do nothing with it, they do not realize that they are all-powerful, with the result that the catastrophe is delayed and the castle of Walhalla, insecure but glorious, fronts the storms for generations. Fafnir, coiled around his hoard, grumbles and grunts; we can hear him under Europe today; the leaves of the wood already tremble, and the Bird calls its warnings uselessly. Fafnir will destroy us, but by a blessed dispensation he is stupid and slow, and creation goes on just outside the poisonous blast of his breath. The Nietzschean would hurry the monster up, the mystic would say he didn't exist, but Wotan, wiser than either, hastens to create warriors before doom declares itself. The Valkyries are symbols not only of courage but of intelligence; they represent the human spirit snatching its opportunity while the going is good, and one of them must be accepted as true if we are to go on the recurrence of love, and since it is the privilege of art to exaggerate she goes even further, and proclaims the love which is eternally triumphant and feeds upon freedom, and lives.

So that is what I feel about force and violence. It is, alas! the ultimate reality, on this earth, but—hooray!—it doesn't always get to the front. Some people call its absences "decadence"; I call them "civilization" and find in such interludes the chief justification for the human experiment. I look the other way until fate strikes me. Whether this is due to courage or to cowardice in my own case I cannot be sure. But I know that if men hadn't looked the other way in the past nothing of any value would survive. The people I respect most behave as if they were immortal and as if society were eternal. Both assumptions are false: both of them must be accepted as true if we are to go on eating and working and loving, and are to keep open a few breathing holes for the human spirit. No millennium seems likely to descend upon humanity; no better and stronger League of Nations will be instituted; no form of Christianity and no alternative to Christianity will bring peace to the world or integrity to the individual; no "change of heart" will occur. And yet we needn't despair, indeed we cannot despair; the evidence of history shows us that men have always insisted on behaving creatively under the shadow of the sword; that they have done their artistic and scientific and domestic stuff for the sake of doing it, and that we had better follow their example under the shadow of the airplanes. Others, with more vision or courage than myself, see the salvation of humanity ahead, and will dismiss my conception of civilization as paltry, a sort of tip-and-run game. Certainly it is presumptuous to say that we _can't_ improve, and that man, who has only been in power for a few thousand years, will never learn to make use of his power. All I mean is that, if people continue to kill one another at the rate they do, the world cannot get better than it is, and that since there are more people than formerly, and their means for destroying one another more diabolic, the world may well get worse. What's good in people— and consequently in the world—is their insistence on creation, their belief in friendship, in loyalty, for its own sake; and though violence remains and is indeed the major partner in this muddled establishment, I believe that creativeness remains too, and will always assume direction when violence sleeps. So, though I am not an optimist, I cannot agree with Sophocles that it were better never to have been born. And although I see no evidence that each batch of births is superior to the last, I leave the field open for this happier view. This is such a difficult time to live in, especially for a European, one can't help getting gloomy and also a bit rattled.

There is of course hero worship, fervently recommended as a panacea in some quarters. But here we shall get no help. Hero worship is a dangerous vice, and one of the minor merits of a democracy is that it does not encourage it, or produce that unmanageable type of citizen known as the Great Man. It produces instead different kinds of small men, and that's a much finer achievement. But people who can't get interested in the variety of life and can't make up their own minds get discontented over this, and they long for a hero to bow down before and to follow blindly. It's significant that a hero is an integral part of the authoritarian stock in trade today. An efficiency regime can't be run without a few heroes stuck about to carry off the dullness—much as plums have to be put into a bad pudding to make it palatable. One hero at the top and a smaller one each side of him is a favorite arrangement, and the timid and the bored are comforted by such a trinity, and, bowing down, feel exalted by it.

No, I distrust Great Men. They produce a desert of uniformity around them and often a pool of blood, too, and I always feel a little man's pleasure when they come a cropper. Every now and then one reads in the newspapers some such statement as, "The *coup d'état* appears to have failed, and Admiral Boga's whereabouts is at present unknown." Admiral Boga had probably every qualification for being a great man—an iron will, personal magnetism, dash, flair—but fate was against him, so he retires to unknown whereabouts instead of parading history with his peers. He fails with a completeness that no artist and no lover can experience, because with them the process of creation is itself an achievement, whereas with him the only possible achievement is success. I believe in aristocracy though—if that's the right word, and if a democrat may use it. Not an aristocracy of power, based upon rank and influence, but an aristocracy of the sensitive, the considerate, and the plucky. Its members are to be found in all nations and classes, and all through the ages, and there is a secret understanding between them when they meet. They represent the true human tradition, the one permanent victory of our queer race over cruelty and chaos. Thousands of them perish in obscurity; a few are great names. They are sensitive for others as well as for themselves, they are considerate without being fussy, their pluck is not swankiness but the power to endure, and they can take a joke. I give no example—it is risky to do that—but the reader may as well consider whether this is the type of person he would like to meet and to be, and whether (going further with me) he would prefer that the type should *not* be an ascetic one. I'm against asceticism myself. I'm with the old Scotchman who wanted less chastity and more delicacy. I don't feel that my aristocrats are a real aristocracy if they thwart their bodies, since bodies are the instruments through which we register and enjoy the world. Still, I don't insist here. This isn't a major point. It's clearly possible to be sensitive, considerate, and plucky and yet be an ascetic too, and if anyone possesses the first three qualities, I'll let him in! On they go—an invincible army, yet not a victorious one. The aristocrats, the elect, the chosen, the best people— all the words that describe them are false, and all attempts to organize them fail. Again and again authority, seeing their value, has tried to net them and to utilize them as the Egyptian priesthood or the Christian Church or the Chinese civil service or the Group Movement, or some other worthy stunt. But they slip through the net and are gone; when the door is shut they are no longer in the room; their temple, as one of them remarked, is the holiness of the heart's imagination, and their kingdom, though they never possess it, is the wide open world.

With this type of person knocking about, and constantly crossing one's path if one has eyes to see or hands to feel, the experiment of earthly life cannot be dismissed as a failure. But it may well be hailed as a tragedy, the tragedy being that no device has been found by which these private decencies can be transferred to public affairs. As soon as people have power they go crooked and sometimes dotty, too, because the possession of power lifts them into a region where normal honesty never pays. For instance, the man who is selling newspapers outside the Houses of Parliament can safely leave his papers to go for a drink, and his cap beside them: anyone who takes a paper is sure to drop a copper into the cap. But the men who are inside the Houses of Parliament—they can't trust one another like that; still less can the government they compose trust other governments. No caps upon the pavement here, but suspicion, treachery, and armaments. The more highly public life is organized the lower does its morality sink; the nations of today behave to each other worse than they ever did in the past, they cheat, rob, bully, and bluff, make war without notice, and kill as many women and children as possible; whereas primitive tribes were at all events restrained by taboos. It's a humiliating outlook—though the greater the darkness, the brighter shine the little lights, reassuring one another, signaling, "Well, at all events I'm still here. I don't like it very much, but how are you?" Unquenchable lights of my aristocracy! Signals of the invincible army! "Come along—anyway let's have a good time while we can." I think they signal that too.

The savior of the future—if ever he comes—will not preach a new gospel. He will merely utilize my aristocracy; he will make effective the good will and the good temper which are already existing. In other words he will introduce a new technique. In economics, we are told that if there was a new technique of distribution, there need be no poverty, and people would not starve in one place while crops were dug under in another. A similar change is needed in the sphere of morals and politics. The desire for it is by no means new; it was expressed, for example, in theological terms by Jacopone da Todi over six hundred years ago. *"Ordina questo amore, O tu che m'ami,"* he said. "O thou who lovest me—set this love in order."· His prayer was not granted and I do not myself believe that it ever will be, but here, and not through a change of heart, is our probable route. Not by becoming better, but by ordering and distributing his native goodness, will man shut up force into his box, and so gain time to explore the universe and to set his mark upon it worthily. At present he only explores it at odd moments, when force is looking the other way, and his divine creativeness appears as a trivial by-product, to be scrapped as soon as the drums beat and the bombers hum.

Such a change, claim the orthodox, can only be made by Christianity, and will be made by it in God's good time: man always has failed and always will fail to organize his own goodness, and it is presumptuous of him to try. This claim—solemn as it is—leaves me cold. I cannot believe that Christianity will ever cope with the present worldwide mess, and I think that such influence as it retains in modern society is due to its financial backing rather than to its spiritual appeal. It was a spiritual force once, but the indwelling spirit will have to be restated if it is to calm the waters again, and probably restated in a non-Christian form. Naturally a great many people, and people who are not only good but able and intelligent, will disagree with me here; they will vehemently deny that Christianity has failed, or they will argue that its failure proceeds from the wickedness of men, and really proves its ultimate success. They have Faith, with a large F. My faith has a very small one, and I only bring it into the open because these are strenuous and serious days, and one likes to say what one thinks while speech is still free: it may not be free much longer.

These are the reflections of an individualist and a liberal who has found his liberalism crumbling beneath him and at first felt ashamed. Then, looking around, he decided there was no special reason for shame, since other people, whatever they felt, were equally insecure. And as for individualism—there seems no way out of this, even if one wants to find one. The dictator-hero can grind down his citizens till they are all alike, but he can't melt them into a single man. That is beyond his power. He can order them to merge, he can incite them to mass antics, but they are obliged to be born separately and to die separately and, owing to these unavoidable termini, will always be running off the totalitarian rails. The memory of birth and the expectation of death always lurk within the human being, making him separate from his fellows and consequently capable of intercourse with them. Naked I came into the world, naked I shall go out of it! And a very good thing too, for it reminds me that I am naked under my shirt. Until psychologists and biologists have done much more tinkering than seems likely, the individual remains firm and each of us must consent to be one, and to make the best of the difficult job.

Can We Survive the Fun Explosion?

by Joseph Wood Krutch

A social commentator looks at our times and questions the future of a world in which fun and violence coexist and where people are willing to forget the past and what it has to teach the present.

Stern censors usually denounce their contemporaries as "pleasure-mad." Our age being one when sociology gets more attention than the fulminations of the moralist, the preferred term is "fun-oriented." For although this term is also sometimes pejorative, it is not always so. A few years ago, for example, Daniel Lerner published in the *American Scholar* an article not explicitly taking sides but giving a very tolerant description of the "fun-oriented" society.

"The theory that every man has a right to comfortable conditions of life is," he said, "the economic counterpart of the theory that every man has the right to be continuously entertained. . . . The old Puritan ethic (or perhaps, more exactly, simply Protestant), with its emphasis on effort, achievement, struggle, and success, has yielded to a whole new array of words expressing the new concept of right conduct and a good life."

About the same time Miss Katherine Hoskins, writing in the *Hudson Review*, took a more positive stand: "I sometimes think that our volatility, our lack of memory, our wastefulness, and other qualities that seem weaknesses could be the virtues of two hundred years from now. I can imagine a new ethos, a different hierarchy of values into which our characteristic would fit. . . . A world more fluid, more abstract—where all things are easily picked up, easily put down. A world without monuments and where one didn't save string, an era of present rationality and charm, wherein the ego has learned grace and poetry and uses them."

Now it is true that there are distinctions between what being "pleasure-mad" on the one hand and "fun-oriented" on the other implies. "Pleasure-mad" suggests dissipation accompanied by the search for madder music and stronger wine. "Fun-oriented" sometimes suggests only golf, picnics, cook-outs, and all sorts of innocent happenings. Still, one does shade into the other.

It has always seemed to me strange that the left-wingers who despise the "privileged class" and find no virtue except in "the worker" should suppose that if everybody had the equivalent of inherited wealth everybody would be fine. The rich playboy has always been an irritating phenomenon, but in the past he was never numerous enough to constitute a serious problem. Many members of the middle and lower classes now enjoy the "privileges" that were once abused by the rich only, and maybe that is why the youth problem grows. At least this seems as reasonable a theory as the more popular opposite, which is that society deprives too large a proportion of its members of the goods they have the right to expect. As a Tory might say, "They seemed to behave better when they had even less."

A few days ago I stood on a busy streetcorner in Tucson watching the young people go by and asking myself if I saw in them the emergence of the new and healthily fun-oriented type. I concluded that the first step (if it really is in that direction) had obviously been taken. Physically, they were a healthier-looking, more confident lot than one is likely to see in any other country. Among the young women (in whom of course I was most interested) there may have been few who could be singled out as great beauties, but the level of physical attractiveness was certainly high—and obviously high on the list of their ambitions. Since their models were those of the movies, the television screen, and the fan magazines, the almost universal effect aimed at was that of the siren—the dangerous woman, or what Hollywood calls, somewhat inelegantly, the "sexpot." But this was despite the fact that few of them had the temperament to go with this outward show or were capable of fulfilling the promises their appearance seemed to hold out. Instead of going on to a career of devastation, most of them are destined to end up in a few years pushing a cart in the supermarket—the cart being used as transportation for one or more "kids" until such time as the space they are occupying is needed for canned baby food. Though their heads will be crowned by large curlers they will be definitely "fun-oriented" rather than "pleasure-mad."

In one other respect I think I can see, even in the faces of the youngest, that they are also already living in that new world "where all things are easily picked up and put down" and where there are no "monuments." Translated, this means that they have gladly accepted our "civilization of the disposable," in which everything from Kleenex to automobiles is to be casually discarded and in which, instead of looking for a usable past, they are so completely unaware that any past exists that they have no need to reject it. They really were "born yesterday" and the last thing that would ever occur to them would be to familiarize themselves with the best that has been thought and said. Their beauty (if you can call it by so exalted a term) is the exact opposite of what Pater thought he saw in the Mona Lisa. None of the sorrows of the world has come to rest on their faces and if the eyelids are a little weary that is only because their owners were up late last night having fun.

If you assume (as they unconsciously do) that there is no such thing as the wisdom of the ages and that there is nothing to be learned from even the mistakes of the past, then perhaps they are right in being happily ignorant of it. But I find it hard to believe that the slate should be wiped quite so clean.

Presently I found myself thinking, in my old-fashioned way, about Matthew Arnold's classification of his contemporaries, and I think that it requires some modification if it is to be applied this hundred years later. What he called the cultured are perhaps as numerous (which is also as few) as they were in his time. But if I understand aright another of his distinctions, there are fewer Philistines and more Barbarians, i.e., fewer who have rejected culture and chosen vulgarity, more who are simply unaware that culture exists. The values of the Philistine—comfort, money, and power—are consciously held and therefore not wholly unexamined. His thinking may be vulgar and directed toward the achievement of vulgar ends but it is at least thinking of a sort, and the choices are deliberately made. The Barbarian does not really think or choose at all with his conscious mind. He merely finds himself living in a world of physical sensations, quite unaware that any other existence is possible. I know that we spend millions on schools, that no other nation is so supplied with libraries, that paperbacks proliferate, and that even TV devotes hours to "education." But I have the feeling that a very large number of youths of both sexes are as untouched by all this as though it did not exist.

In addition to Arnold's categories one must of course establish a new one either nonexistent or unnamed in Arnold's day: the category of the Alienated. This category includes two subdivisions, into one or the other of which the existentialist and the beatnik are placed. Both have one thing in common with the Philistine because both have rejected "culture" in Arnold's sense, though they often know more about it than his Philistines did. They differ from one another in that the highly intellectual existentialist is depressed while the beatnik has taken only one step away from the fun-oriented society and finds the *summum bonum* to be not fun but "kicks."

Lytton Strachey once remarked that when Victorians "lost their faith" they reacted to the loss in different ways. To some it was merely a burden laid down; to others it was more as though they had lost a portmanteau that they continued to look nervously about for. The beatnik and the existentialist react in a somewhat analogous manner to their own loss of faith in the whole system of beliefs and values of the Western world. And to me the discouraging fact is that if, as seems to be the case, the existentialists will be the teachers of any Barbarians who decide to live "an examined life" instead of an unexamined one, there isn't too much to choose between the two. In fact, I am inclined to think that I would rather live among the modern Barbarians than in a society really dominated by the completely alienated—whether existentialist or beatnik.

For those of us who live in the United States our world is almost completely without monuments in the literal as well as in the figurative sense, and I wonder if this absence of physical monuments does not encourage our unawareness of the monuments of thought and feeling in which the Barbarians refuse to interest themselves. When (as seems to be increasingly the case) the schools make a halfhearted effort to call some attention to them, we, so the pupils reply, are "modern" and we can't be bothered with what ought to have been disposed of long ago. In many schools, it seems, the attempt to present culture has been given up in despair, "assigned reading" now being any book the pupil cares to choose—with the result that, so I am told, one class in a Tucson high school is "studying" *Peyton Place.*

Even in New York there are few physical objects outside museums to remind anyone of the fact that the city has a past; and to the Barbarian a museum (which he does not often visit) is the only proper place for anything that was made more than twenty years ago. Buildings are not disposed of quite as quickly as automobiles (just as automobiles are not disposed of as quickly as Kleenex), but there is little desire to keep any of them long. What a fanatical antiquarian called "vandalism" we call "modernization." As a result, even the most ambitious public structures are almost in the class of consumer goods, with the stress on "consumer" and by consequence on consumption.

I am told that even the Parisian is losing interest in his "monuments" and is quite reconciled to seeing them replaced by modern structures of either the glass-box or the Corbusier variety. Yet of all great cities his is the one in which monuments of both the remote and the recent past are most conspicuously integrated into the whole city to which they contribute so much of its character. These monuments are lived in and with, not merely preserved. Hence the citizen does not have to seek them out but passes Notre Dame, the Louvre, and the Arc de Triomphe—each a characteristic monument of some part of his past—as he goes about his business or pleasure. In New York the most you are likely to find is the plaque that says, "On this spot once stood . . ."

I do not think it is mere prejudice that has led me to believe that the man and woman on the Paris street look somehow aware of more things than do their opposite numbers in Tucson or New York, and if this is not an illusion then it may be that their physical city has something to do with the fact. Of course, they also look less healthy, physically less imposing, and I am certain that the American would not want to give up his advantage there in exchange for what the Parisian seems to have. But is a choice really necessary?

A few years ago Robert Graves gave a speech before the American Academy of Arts and Letters, the subject of which was announced mysteriously as "On the Word *Baraka.*" It turned out that this word is Arabic and refers to that particular charm (in both the literal and figurative senses of the word) which adheres to anything from a cooking pot to a mosque that has been long used either by an individual or his clan. Mr. Graves's point was that we rarely keep anything, cooking pot or building, long enough for it to acquire even a trace of this charm and that the central fact of our civilization is that we prefer newness to *baraka.* My objection to the new Utopia certainly includes the fact that the very concept of *baraka* will have been forgotten.

Is it—or isn't it—a cause for surprise that the age of fun should be also both an age of violence and (among a conspicuous group of intellectuals) an age of philosophical despair? Fun, violence, and despair seem at first sight to make an unexpected trio but perhaps there is a natural relation. Since you can't possibly have fun all the time, since seeking it too persistently and too exclusively is a sure way of finding boredom and frustration instead, perhaps pessimism is the inevitable reaction of the thoughtful, and violence the inevitable reaction of those who do not analyze their frustrations.

If it is true that the American family spends an average of five hours a day watching television, then what it is so doggedly exposing itself to must indicate something about the inner life of its members. The seeming incongruity of the fun-oriented commercial that usually interrupts the most sadistic spectacle again calls attention to the kinship between the two. Suddenly at some climax of violence comes the "word from our sponsor." What one logically expects is an offer of heroin, of brass knuckles sent COD "in a plain wrapper," or, possibly, some direction for obtaining police protection. But the advertiser assumes that what the audience wants most is something that will keep its hair in place or get the clothes really white. Are these two things—the sadistic melodrama on the one hand and the commercial on the other—the two competing versions of the American dream and is it the triviality of the one that creates an appetite for thrills and excitement at any cost?

What cannot be doubted is the all too obvious fact that this is indeed an age of violence, both public and private. Publicly, it is an age of revolutions, small wars, and riots; privately, an age of vandalism and brutal assaults that suggest the "unmotivated act" of the existentialist novel, though the perpetrator usually can give no such rationalized explanation. When, a few months ago, a Tucson youth drove an icepick into the back of a school maintenance worker and then said he had no idea why he assaulted a man against whom he had no grudge, the shocking thing was that, in a sense, the incident was too typical of what one reads about almost daily to cause shock. And one wonders again if the reaction against the boredom of a fun-oriented society does not have something to do with the situation.

The New York World's Fair adopted as its theme "Man's Achievements in an Expanding Universe" but its theme song (to the music of Richard Rodgers) is: "Walk away from every care/This is your fun time/you are entitled to it." Walking away from every care in an expanding universe may seem to require some doing, but isn't that last clause, "you are entitled to it," the real theme song of our society? Did the natural right to *pursue* happiness become somehow the right to *get* happiness and did that right inevitably degenerate into a right to have fun—for the simple reason that the impossibility of guaranteeing fun is less obvious than the impossibility of guaranteeing happiness? Do children destroy schools and students plunge icepicks into custodians simply because they are not getting the fun they have been told they have a right to and are taking their revenge?

Sociologists used to blame all youthful delinquency and most adult criminality on a society that had deprived the child or the adult of decent conditions of life. But the explanation will no longer hold water. Youthful delinquents and vandals come from every stratum of society—from the poor who have too little, from the rich who have too much, and from the middle classes, which seem to have just the right proportion of the things the sociologists talk about. We can't all belong to the jet set but few of us are too poor to join its lower-income analogue, the motorcycle set. If many at both levels have been deprived, it is not of comfort and material luxuries. Perhaps what they suffer is being deprived of a set of values not to be found in a fun-oriented society. There we are all taught to believe that fun is what everyone has a right to; that if you do not have as much of it as you think you should you are "deprived"; and that to be deprived is to make any protest up to and including murder "understandable" because society, not you, is to blame.

Still another paradox is the fact that this fun-oriented and violence-oriented society is also, on the other hand, playing a leading role in a world movement aimed at extending freedom and equality to all persons within our own country and ultimately to all nations. Perhaps the most tragic consequence of a taste for violence is the extent to which it confuses the motives of every social or political movement, from the demand for civil rights to anticolonial revolution, by making them sometimes genuinely what they profess to be and sometimes merely excuses for violence. Students strike and riot for absurd as well as for legitimate reasons. One is not quite sure whether the inhabitants of Cyprus wanted independence for reasons credible to human dignity or merely in order that Turks and Greeks might indulge in the fun of killing one another; whether a South-eastern confederation wants to be a self-governing nation out of legitimate "national aspirations" or whether the greatest national aspiration is to be strong enough to attack and subdue its neighbors. Surely the unholiest of united fronts is this one formed by the union of those who have a passion for justice with those moved only by a pathological lust to destroy. And it is all the more dangerous because even individuals are sometimes self-deceived.

The apologies for a fun-oriented society seem to assume that security and abundance are automatic as well as permanent and that somehow or other they will continue to bless those who have put "having fun" before everything else. Theirs would be, it seems to me, a rather ignoble

Utopia and it is certainly an impossible one. At this moment one cannot be sure whether we are headed toward a world more just and happier than it has ever been, or whether (as the news of yesterday and today seems often to suggest) toward a dark age where violence, both private and public, is normal and almost continuous. The fun-oriented are not likely to be of much help in settling the question.

Why I Dislike
Western Civilization

by Arnold Toynbee

A British historian criticizes our society because he thinks it creates tyrants, encourages excessive materialism and mismanages the education of its youth.

When I say baldly that I dislike contemporary Western civilization, I am, of course, saying this partly to tease my fellow Westerners. The stand that I take is partly a joke, but it is also partly serious.

My dislike of the West, though genuine as far as it goes, cannot really be unmitigated. If it were, I should not feel lost—as I know that I should—if I did not have a *pied-à-terre* in London. I am a Londoner born and bred, but I have not reacted against my native city; and, though I dislike the congestion of the mechanized traffic there, I know that this pest is just as bad in all the other great cities of the postwar world.

If I were to be hounded out of London by some (nonexistent) British counterpart of the House Committee on Un-American Activities, I expect I could make myself at home in Edinburgh or Melbourne or Rome or Hamburg or Boston, Mass. (my great-grandfather's farm was in sight of Boston Stump, the tapering tower of St. Botolph's Church in Boston, England). I should not feel at home as a permanent resident in New York or Chicago or Pittsburgh or Glasgow or Manchester or Milan. And I do not suppose that I could strike root in Kyoto or in Damascus or in Istanbul or even in Athens, though I love and admire each of these beautiful non-Western cities.

In ancient Greece, the navel of the earth was marked by a monolith at Delphi. The navel of my earth is not in Greece (though my heart and mind reside there). My world-navel is the Albert Memorial in Kensington Gardens.

This British monument may be comically ugly but, to me, it is reassuringly familiar. I used to play around its steps when I was a tiny child. Its frieze taught me the names of the great poets, artists and thinkers of the past; the group of figures at the four corners put the four continents on the map for me.

Yes, one is a prisoner of one's time and place. I belong to the presyncopation age. Classical Western music is music for my ears. When I hear jazz, I become uneasy and turn hostile. I feel my traditional world being victoriously invaded by tropical Africa. Politically, I am on the side of Africa against the Western colonial powers, but when it comes to music, Africa's cultural colonialism makes me cherish the West's pre-African musical past.

To be the prisoner of one's time and place is one of our human limitations. A human being has roots, like a tree, and these roots tether him—though, unlike a tree's roots, they are emotional and intellectual roots. However, it is characteristic of our human nature that we rebel against our human limitations and try to transcend them. I myself, besides being human, happen to be a historian, and a historian's special form of human rebellion is to try to shake himself free of his own parochial blood and soil (to use Hitler's hateful but expressive words). A historian's métier is to move freely through time and space.

What a bore one's own native civilization is. It is dull just because it is familiar. I had the good fortune to be educated in Greek and Latin. This education served me as a magic carpet on which I wafted myself from the twentieth century of the Christian era to the third century B.C., and from the North Atlantic to the Eastern Mediterranean. I hated having to learn the names and dates of the Kings of England. The kings of Israel and Judah were almost as bad, since the Old Testament in the King James version has become virtually part of English literature. But I enjoyed finding my way among the Ptolemies and the Seleucuses. English constitutional history? One glance at the syllabus of the Oxford school of medieval and modern history was enough to put me off reading for that. But the history of Islam, the history of Buddhism—these opened up fascinating new worlds.

Contemporary Western civilization annoys me, not be-

cause it is Western, but because it is mine and because I
am a historian. If I had happened to be born in 1889 in
China instead of England, no doubt I should be annoyed
today with the China of Pu Yi and Chiang Kai-shek and
Chou En-lai. But being, as I am, a Western historian, I
am inevitably annoyed by the contemporary West. It holds
me fast entangled in its coils. It prevents me from getting
back behind the machine age and from getting out into Russia, Dar-el-Islam, the Hindu world, Eastern Asia. My inescapable Westernness makes it impossible for me to become
culturally acclimatized in any of these other contemporary
civilizations. This is a limitation on my human freedom
that I resent.

However, I have a more formidable reason for disliking
the West than any that I have mentioned so far. Since I
have been grown-up (I am now turned 75), the West has
produced two world wars; it has produced Communism,
Fascism and National Socialism; it has produced Mussolini
and Hitler and McCarthy. These Western enormities make
me, as a Westerner, feel insecure. Now that my German
fellow-Westerners have murdered six million Jews, how
can I be certain that my English fellow-countrymen might
not do something equally criminal? We did murder some
thousands of defenseless civilians at Port Said in 1956.
What might we not go on to do after that? What might I
not be capable of doing myself, if this contemporary
Western criminal lunacy were to waylay me?

I shiver and shake. Old-fashioned Christian humility,
please come to my rescue. Please save me from contemporary post-Christian Western self-complacent sinfulness. I
should feel my spirits rise if, instead of being Hitler's fellow-Westerner—as I am—I could be Gandhi's fellow-Hindu.
Yes, I believe I could even stomach Benares as the price
of being liberated from Hitler's company. But I cannot escape Hitler. This fellow-Westerner of mine (of the same age
to within a week) is going to haunt me for the rest of my
West-bound life.

Apart from contemporary Western crimes, there are other
blemishes on contemporary Western life that I find repul-
sive. Though I dislike the former enslavement of the individual to the community in Japan, I also dislike, and this
perhaps even more, the lengths to which contemporary West-

ern individualism has gone. The contemporary West is callous toward the aged. This is, I believe, the first civilization, so far, in which the aged have not had a place, as a matter of course, in their adult children's homes. Looking at this Western callousness with de-Westernized eyes, I find it shocking.

I also dislike the contemporary Western advertising business. It has made a fine art out of taking advantage of human silliness. It rams unwanted material goods down surfeited throats when two-thirds of all human beings now alive are in desperate need of the bare necessities of life. This is an ugly aspect of the affluent society; and, if I am told that advertising is the price of affluence, I reply without hesitation, that affluence has been bought too dear. Another item in the price of affluence is the standardization of mass-produced goods and services. This is, in itself, a deplorable impoverishment of the material side of human culture, and it brings spiritual standardization with it, which is still worse.

Looking back into the past history of the West—a past which was still present when I was a child—I admire the nineteenth-century West's success in postponing the age of sexual awakening, of sexual experience and sexual infatuation far beyond the age of physical puberty. You may tell me that this was against nature; but to be human consists precisely in transcending nature—in overcoming the biological limitations that we have inherited from our prehuman ancestors.

All human societies overcome death by creating and maintaining institutions that are handed on from one generation to another. Sex is a still more awkward feature of our biological inheritance than death, and our nineteenth-century Western society handled sex with relative success. By postponing the age of sexual awakening, it prolonged the length of the period of education. It is this, together with the seventeenth-century Western achievement of learning to think for oneself instead of taking tradition on trust, that accounts for the West's preeminence in the world during the last few centuries.

Nineteenth-century Westerners condemned with justice the Hindu institution of child-marriage, and they deplored, also with justice, the spectacle of an intellectually promising Moslem boy being allowed to commit intellectual suicide by sexual indulgence at the age of puberty. The twentieth-century West is now imitating the non-Western habits that the nineteenth-century West rightly—though perhaps self-righteously—condemned.

Our irrational contemporary Western impatience and our blind adulation of speed for speed's sake are making havoc, today, of the education of our children. We force their growth as if they were chicks in a pullet factory. We drive them into a premature awareness of sex even before physical puberty has overtaken them. In fact, we deprive our children of the human right of having a childhood. This forcing of sex-consciousness started in the United States; it has spread to Britain, and who knows how many other Western countries this perverse system of miseducation is going to invade and demoralize?

Our whole present policy in the upbringing of the young is paradoxical. While we are lowering the age of sexual awareness—and frequently the age of sexual experience, too—to a veritably Hindu degree, we are at the same time prolonging the length of education. We force our boys and girls to become sex-conscious at twelve or thirteen, and then we ask them to prolong their postgraduate studies till they are nearly thirty. How are they to be expected to give their minds to education during those last sixteen or seventeen sex-haunted years?

We are proud of ourselves for providing secondary education, college education, postgraduate education for everybody. But we shall be plowing the sands if we do not simultaneously revert to our grandparents' practice of prolonging the age of sexual innocence. If we persist, in this vital matter, on our present Hindu course, our brand-new would-be institutions for higher education will become, in practice, little more than social clubs for sexual mating.

This relapse into precocious sexuality is one of the moral blemishes of the contemporary Western civilization. One of its intellectual blemishes is its insistence on splitting up the universe into smaller and smaller splinters. It has split up the human race into a host of sovereign independent national states. It has split up knowledge and understanding into a host of separate watertight "disciplines." I dislike nationalism and I dislike specialization, and both are characteristically Western aberrations.

When I was about sixteen years old, I stayed with an uncle who was a specialist on Dante, while his wife was a specialist on Horace Walpole. Their library was less specialized than they themselves were, and I browsed in it with excitement and delight. When I was due to leave, my uncle said to me: "Arnold, your aunt and I think you are allowing your interest to be too general. You ought to specialize." I said nothing, but I was instantaneously certain that I was not going to follow this advice; and, in fact, I have consistently done the opposite throughout the sixty years that have passed since then.

What a world to find oneself born into. Since as early as I first became conscious of my native Western environment, Western technology has been inventing new and ever more complicated machines. I did learn to ride a bicycle. How can one be expected, in just one lifetime, to go on to learn to ride a motorcycle or to drive a car? I started shaving in the age of the cutthroat razor, and Mr. Gillette's invention came as a great relief to me. But how can I be expected to go on to use an electric razor? How could I know about volts and ohms and transformers? An American friend did give me an electric razor. This lies safely tucked away in a drawer, and whenever I unearth it, it alarms me.

I do now travel about the world in cars and airplanes. The better these get at covering the distance, the worse they get at allowing an inquisitive passenger to see the view. I did my first traveling in Greece in 1911–12. I did it on foot with a rucksack on my back. I was as free as a bird. I could go where even mules could not go. I could see the world as I pleased. I have never traveled so satisfactorily as that since then.

The other day, I had a three-hour mule ride from an airstrip to the rock-cut churches at Lalibela in Ethiopia. Once again I was seeing the real world, the unmechanized pre-Western world in which I feel truly at home. Machinery perplexes and dismays me, and I have been born into the Western machine age. Why was I not born in the third-century-B.C. Syria or seventh-century-A.D. China? I should not then have been harassed by machinery as I am in the contemporary West. I heartily dislike this side of contemporary Western life, and, in the eyes of the rest of the world, mechanization is what the contemporary West stands for.

Well, these are some of the reasons why I dislike the contemporary Western civilization. But, as I have said at the beginning of this article, my dislike is not undiluted. My grandchildren, after all, are Westerners, and I certainly like them. Moreover, I want them, in their turn, to have grandchildren who will have grandchildren. I should be desolated if I believed that Western man was going to commit mass suicide by engaging in a third world war that, this time, would be fought with atomic weapons.

To discover the existence of the atom and to go on to discover how to split it has been the *chef d'oeuvre* of Western science and technology. I do not love Western science for having made these deadly inventions; but I have just enough faith in Western man's political commonsense to expect that he will not liquidate himself. So perhaps, after all, I do not rate my native Western civilization so low as I fancy that I do in my moments of acute exasperation at the West's more uncongenial vagaries.

Fire Walking in Ceylon

by Leonard Feinberg

An American college professor witnesses an ancient Eastern ritual of faith and comments on Western civilization by outlining its attempts to explain the ritual rationally.

Although we had seen men walking barefoot on burning embers twice before, we were not prepared for the mass fire walk at Kataragama. The first time, on a pleasant summer afternoon, surrounded by playing children and laughing family groups, we watched four men walk quickly through a twelve-foot fire pit. The occasion was a Hindu festival, and the atmosphere was similar to that of a state fair in the United States. The second time we had been among the guests of a Ceylonese planter who included in the evening's entertainment a fire-walking exhibition by six men.

But at the temple of Kataragama everything was different. There, on the night of the full moon in August, fire walking climaxes a week's ceremonies in honor of the Hindu god Kataragama. From all over the island, worshipers and spectators (Buddhist as well as Hindu, although theoretically Buddhists do not believe in gods) had been converging on the little settlement in the jungle of southeastern Ceylon. During the early part of the week, devotees had paid tribute to Kataragama by hanging colored papers on trees near the temple or by breaking sacrificial coconuts on a rock provided for that purpose. Toward the week's end, the nature of the sacrifices was intensified, and zealous worshipers perforated their cheeks with pins, or walked on nails, or imbedded into their naked shoulders meathooks with which they pulled heavy carts along a pitted dirt road.

By midnight the crowd was feverishly tense. Since the logs in the twenty-by-six-foot pit had been burning for four hours, the fire walking would presumably take place about 4 A.M. But the tradition against making any sort of prediction about the immediate future is so strong at Kataragama that the local priest, asked by an American tourist when the fire walking would begin, replied that there probably would not be any walking at all. The crowd surged away from the pit slowly and steadily—slowly because every inch of the temple grounds had been packed for hours, and steadily because the heat from the pit was becoming unbearable. The men and women nearest the pit had held their places for days, eating and sleeping in one spot. The Ceylonese are ordinarily very clean, but the activity at Kataragama is more important than sanitation, and as the hours passed everything intensified: the heat, the tension, the odors of sweat and urine and incense. A wave of malevolent expectation permeated the air, a powerful undercurrent of suppressed sadism that made intruders like ourselves feel dilettantish, uncomfortable, and slightly ashamed. Fire walking is far more than just a spectacle to most of these people; it is a concrete symbol of intimate identification with a supernatural power. From time to time men would shout, "Hora Hora," an Oriental form of "Amen" in honor of the god whose power transcends the science of the West.

About 2 A.M. people near us suddenly scurried to make room for a young woman carrying in her bare hands a clay pot full of burning coconut husks. She did not seem to be feeling any pain, but she was abnormally excited as she staggered to the outer sanctum of the temple. There she threw the pot down, exultantly showed the crowd her hands—they were gray, but not burned—and began knocking on the temple door. She apparently wanted to demonstrate to the priest, or the god, what she had accomplished, but no one was being admitted that night, and she was still pounding frantically at the massive door when the attention of the crowd shifted to another woman. This one too had a red-hot pot full of burning husks, but she carried it in the conventional Ceylonese fashion—on top of her head. And when she removed the pot, neither her hair nor her hands showed any sign of scorching.

Shortly before four o'clock an ominous grumbling swept through the crowd. Then angry shouts, threatening arms, protests. By climbing a stone wall I was able to see what the trouble was. A row of chairs had been reserved for several wealthy Ceylonese from Colombo and their Euro-

pean guests. But when they arrived they found that a group
of Buddhist monks had occupied the seats and refused to
move. (For more than a year, as a calculated technique
of growing nationalism, monks had been usurping reserved
seats at public gatherings.) The police officer tried to persuade the monks to give up the seats, but the yellow-robed
figures leaned placidly on their umbrellas and pretended that
he did not exist. There was no question where the sympathy
of the mob lay, and when their protests became loud the
police officer shrugged his shoulders and motioned to the
legal holders of the seats. They dispersed to the edges of
the standing mob, far away from the pit.

At four in the morning wailing flutes and pounding drums
announced the arrival of the walkers. The long procession
was led by white-robbed priests, their faces streaked with
red and yellow and white ash. By this time the flames had
stopped spurting and the pit consisted of a red-hot mass of
burning wood, which attendants were leveling with long
branches. The heat of the fire was still intense; within ten
feet of the pit it was difficult to breathe. Then the priests
muttered incantations, the drums built up to a crescendo,
and the fire walking began.

Among the eighty persons who walked the fire that
night there were ten women. But in the mad excitement
of the crowd's cheers, the drumbeats, the odors, the tension, it was difficult to identify individuals. Some men
skipped lightly through the fire, as if doing a restrained
version of the hop, skip, and jump in three or four steps.
Some raced through, determined, somber. Some ran
through exultantly, waving spears. One man danced gaily
into the center of the pit, turned, did a kind of wild jig
for a few moments, then turned again and danced on
through. Another man stumbled suddenly and the crowd
gasped; he fell forward, hung for a ghastly moment on
the coals, then straightened and stumbled on. The crowd
sighed. Two women ran through, close together, holding
hands, taking five or six steps. In the phantasmagoric blur
of roars, screams, and incantations, the fire walkers looked
less like human beings than grotesque puppets in a macabre
shadow play. For a long moment one person stood out in
the hectic cavalcade of charging, gyrating figures: a short,
slim man in a white sarong strolled slowly and serenely

through the fire, stepping on the solid earth at the end of the pit as gently as he had stepped on the embers.

After going through the fire, the walkers, some shuffling, some running, a few helped or led by attendants, proceeded to a spot beside the temple where the head priest placed a smear of a saffron ash on the forehead of each participant. The ash had been taken from the pit and blessed, and the fire walkers strode off proudly.

There are two types of fire walking, on stones (usually of volcanic origin) in Polynesia, and on embers in Asia and Africa. Theories which try to explain the secret of fire walking fall into three categories: physical, psychological, and religious. The most publicized attempts of scientists to find the solution took place in 1935 and 1936, when the London Council for Psychical Investigation arranged two series of fire walks at Surrey, England. The council took charge of building the pit and burning the logs, it provided a number of physicians, chemists, physicists, and Oxford professors to examine every stage of the proceedings, and it published an official report of its conclusions. Some of the scientists published individual reports, in general agreeing that fire walking can be explained in terms of certain physical facts, but they did not agree on precisely what those physical facts were.

At the first series of Surrey tests, an Indian named Kuda Bux walked uninjured through a fire pit the surface temperature of which was 430° C., the interior temperature 1400° C. In the 1936 test, for Ahmed Hussain, the surface temperature was over 500° C. Both Bux and Hussain insisted that the secret was "faith," and Hussain claimed that he could convey immunity to anyone who would walk the fire with him. A half-dozen English amateurs, who had answered the council's advertisement for volunteers, did walk the fire behind Hussain and were "slightly burned." One of these amateurs managed, a few days later, to walk through the fire pit alone, in three steps, without suffering the slightest injury.

In brief, the official report of the council stated that fire walking is a gymnastic feat operating on this principle: a limited number of quick and even steps on a poor conductor of heat does not result in burning of the flesh.

"The secret of fire-walking," the report said, "lies in the low thermal conductivity of the burning wood. . . . The quantity of heat transferred may remain small, if . . . the time of contact is very short. . . . The time of contact is not above half a second in normal quick walking." To put it another way, it is safe to take three even steps, limiting each contact to half a second, on wood embers ("The thermal conductivity of copper . . . is about 1,000 times greater than that of wood"). The report conceded that "successive contacts . . . cause an accumulation of heat sufficient to cause injury, and . . . with fires whose temperature is 500° Centigrade or more, only two contacts can be made with each foot without erythema or blistering."

The weight of the walker makes a difference, the report suggested, each of the Indians weighing less than 126 pounds and sinking into the embers to a lesser degree, and for a shorter time, than the heavier English amateurs. An expert also has the advantage of walking steadily and distributing his weight evenly, whereas the inexperience and undue haste of the beginner make it difficult for him to avoid resting a part of his foot more heavily than he should. When the amateur walker took an uneven number of steps, the foot which had taken more steps suffered more burns.

Other observers of fire walking have offered various explanations, the most popular being that Orientals have very tough soles. They walk barefoot all their lives, often on hot surfaces. Sometimes they put out cigarette butts with their toes and, when marching in parades, step on burning husks which have fallen out of torchbearers' fires. This is true. But the English physicians who examined Bux and Hussain described their feet as very soft, not at all callused.

Another familiar conjecture is that fire walkers use chemical preparations to protect their feet. An American magician believes that a paste of alum and salt is applied, and other experts have speculated that soda, or soap, or juice of mysterious plants, or an anesthetic of some sort is used. But the physician and the chemist who examined Bux and Hussain at Surrey were positive that nothing had been applied to the feet; for control purposes, they washed one of Bux's feet and dried it carefully before he walked.

The "water-vapor protection" theory has a number of supporters. An American chemist recently wrote, in a popular magazine, that he could walk comfortably on burning coals and apply his tongue painlessly to a red-hot iron bar by utilizing this principle: at a certain range of high temperature, a thin film of water acts as absolute protection against heat. The trouble with this theory, as the Surrey tests showed, is (1) the fire walkers' feet were dry, (2) it would be difficult, under any conditions, to supply a uniform amount of water to the soles during a fire walk, and (3) moisture is not advisable, because embers are likely to stick to wet soles and cause blisters.

Still another explanation was offered by Joseph Dunninger. He asserts that the trick used by fire-walking Shinto priests in Japan consisted of making the fuel in the trench shallow in the center and deep on the sides, and starting the fire in the center. By the time the walking begins, the fire has burned out in the center, is still blazing at the edges, and the priests step on the cool ashes of the center. That may be the secret of the Shinto priests, but the pit at Surrey was filled evenly under the supervision of scientists. And an English planter in the Marquesas Islands, who was once teased by a local chief into fire walking, reported that the fire was hottest in the center.

These are the physical explanations. The psychological theories are more difficult to test. Having watched fire walking in Japan some years ago, Percival Lowell of Harvard concluded that the feat was made possible by the less sensitive nervous organism of the Oriental and the ecstasy of the walker (as well as the extremely tough calluses on his soles). A variation on the "ecstasy" theory is the suggestion of one psychologist that hypnosis is the secret. The fire walker, he says, has been hypnotized and provided with the same immunity to pain that can be observed even in a classroom demonstration of hypnosis. The fire walker may not know that he is hypnotized, but hypnosis is what the priest is actually practicing when he gives the walker his last-minute instructions. After the performance, while ostensibly putting a mark of holy ash on the fire walker's forehead, the priest breaks the hypnosis.

Most psychologists, however, reject this explanation on the grounds that hypnosis may lessen the subjective feeling of pain but cannot prevent skin from burning.

It is well known in the East that yogis and fakirs can attain so profound a state of concentration on a single object that nothing else distracts them. In this state, the practitioner may lie on a bed of nails, keep a hand outstretched for days, remain motionless for a week, or perform other feats whose practical value is limited but which do demonstrate a control over the body that most human beings are unable to achieve. According to some yogis, he who masters concentration can separate the soul from the body, so that the vacant shell does not feel pain. But since a dead body will burn, this explanation is not satisfactory.

As far as the devout Ceylonese believer is concerned, the secret is simple: complete faith in Kataragama. Kataragama is a very powerful god. If, in desperation—at a time of serious illness, near-bankruptcy, dangerous competition from a hated rival—a man or woman vows to walk the fire in exchange for Kataragama's help, Kataragama may give that help. The amateur walker, then, is either a petitioner for supernatural assistance or a grateful recipient of it. His preparation may begin as early as May, when he arrives at Kataragama and puts himself under the direction of the chief priest. For three months he lives ascetically, abstaining from all sensual pleasures, eating only vegetables, drinking only water, bathing in the holy river near the temple, and going through religious rituals conducted by the priest. If he does all this, and if he has *absolute, unquestioning, complete* faith in Kataragama's power, he walks the fire unafraid and unharmed.

On the night we watched the fire walking at Kataragama, twelve people were burned badly enough to go to the hospital, and one of them died. These people, the devout believer will tell you, lacked either faith or preparation. Another man who lacked at least one of these ingredients was a young English clergyman who visited Ceylon a few years ago. This Protestant minister reasoned that the faith of a Christian was at least as strong as that of a

Hindu, and he volunteered to walk the fire with the others. He did, and spent the next six months in a hospital, where doctors barely managed to save his life.

It is believed by the Ceylonese that Kataragama exercises absolute and somewhat whimsical control of the area within a fourteen-mile radius of his temple. His portrait, presumably life-size, shows a handsome, seven-foot-tall, six-headed and twelve-armed god, with two women and a blue peacock for companionship and transportation. Although he is technically a Hindu god, many Buddhists also worship him, or at least ask for his help when they are in trouble. Officially the god of war and revenge, he is probably more fervently worshiped and more genuinely feared than any other god in Ceylon. He has an A-1 reputation for protecting his congregation and, according to numerous legends, exhibits a genial playfulness in devising disconcerting mishaps for those who violate his minor taboos.

Most Ceylonese try to make at least one visit a year to his temple, not necessarily during the August ceremonies, but at some other time of the year when the settlement in the jungle is sparse, quiet, and suitable for meditation. Everyone manages to get to Kataragama sooner or later, it seems. My Hindu friend in the police department went one week, my wife's Muslim jeweler another, my Buddhist tailor a third. It is considered especially commendable to walk all the way to Kataragama, and many Ceylonese do walk there, sometimes carrying a large, colorful, paper-and-wood contraption in the form of an arch, which indicates that they are fulfilling a vow.

Our driver on the trip to Kataragama was a young Singhalese who told us that his name was Elvis. (He told Englishmen that his name was Winston.) His driving got a little erratic as the day wore on, and he finally admitted that, though a Buddhist, he was taking no chances with Kataragama and had been fasting all day. While we were eating, he warned our friends and us about certain taboos that visitors to the Kataragama territory were supposed to observe. One local rule forbade announcing an expected arrival time; that, said Elvis, was an infallible way of being delayed. Another dangerous thing to do was to speak disrespectfully of Kataragama. A Buddhist in a

Renault immediately remarked that, the weather being ideal, we ought to arrive at Kataragama by six o'clock. And a Christian woman in a Vauxhall said that all this fear of Kataragama was nonsense; she had been there the previous year and had ridiculed the entire procedure, but nothing had happened.

When we finished eating we got into our Volkswagen and followed the other two cars. Suddenly it began to rain. It rained only for five minutes and, we learned later, only within a few hundred yards. As we carefully rounded a curve on the slick road we saw that the two other cars were now facing us. The Renault's hood was stuck halfway into a rock fence, and the Vauxhall was resting its side on the same fence. It turned out that the Renault had skidded and started turning in the road, and to avoid hitting it the driver of the Vauxhall put on her brakes. By the time the cars stopped skidding they had smashed into the fence. No one was injured except the scoffing woman, who had a painful but not serious bruise on the spot where an irritated parent might have been expected to spank his child. It took a long time to improvise pulling cables, disengage the cars, and tow them to a garage. We eventually reached the temple, just before midnight, and although all of these coincidences and superstitions can be logically accounted for, no one in our party made any more jeering remarks about Kataragama.

One Vote for this Age of Anxiety

by Margaret Mead

An anthropologist differentiates between "good anxiety" and that which is unwarranted, puts our society in its proper historical and geographical context, and suggests that, by facing the inevitability of death, man can achieve dignity.

When critics wish to repudiate the world in which we live today, one of their familiar ways of doing it is to castigate modern man because anxiety is his chief problem. This, they say, in W. H. Auden's phrase, is the age of anxiety. This is what we have arrived at with all our vaunted progress, our great technological advances, our great wealth—everyone goes about with a burden of anxiety so enormous that, in the end, our stomachs and our arteries and our skins express the tension under which we live. Americans who have lived in Europe come back to comment on our favorite farewell which, instead of the old goodbye (God be with you), is now "Take it easy," each American admonishing the other not to break down from the tension and strain of modern life.

Whenever an age is characterized by a phrase, it is presumably in contrast to other ages. If we are the age of anxiety, what were other ages? And here the critics and carpers do a very amusing thing. First, they give us lists of the opposites of anxiety: security, trust, self-confidence, self-direction. Then, without much further discussion, they let us assume that other ages, other periods of history, were somehow the ages of trust or confident direction.

The savage who, on his South Sea island, simply sat and let breadfruit fall into his lap, the simple peasant, at one with the fields he ploughed and the beasts he tended, the craftsman busy with his tools and lost in the fulfillment of the instinct of workmanship—these are the counter-images conjured up by descriptions of the strain under which men live today. But no one who lived in those days has returned to testify how paradisiacal they really were.

Certainly if we observe and question the savages or simple peasants in the world today, we find something quite different. The untouched savage in the middle of New Guinea isn't anxious; he is seriously and continually *frightened*—of black magic, of enemies with spears who may kill him or his wives and children at any moment, while they stoop to drink from a spring, or climb a palm tree for a coconut. He goes warily, day and night, taut and fearful.

As for the peasant populations of a great part of the world, they aren't so much anxious as hungry. They aren't anxious about whether they will get a salary raise, or which of the three colleges of their choice they will be admitted to, or whether to buy a Ford or Cadillac, or whether the kind of TV set they want is too expensive. They are hungry, cold and, in many parts of the world, they dread that local warfare, bandits, political coups may endanger their homes, their meager livelihoods and their lives. But surely they are not anxious.

For anxiety, as we have come to use it to describe our characteristic state of mind, can be contrasted with the active fear of hunger, loss, violence and death. Anxiety is the appropriate emotion when the immediate personal terror—of a volcano, an arrow, the sorcerer's spell, a stab in the back and other calamities, all directed against one's self—disappears.

This is not to say that there isn't plenty to worry about in our world of today. The explosion of a bomb in the streets of a city whose name no one had ever heard before may set in motion forces which end up by ruining one's carefully planned education in law school, half a world away. But there is still not the personal, immediate, active sense of impending disaster that the savage knows. There is rather the vague anxiety, the sense that the future is unmanageable.

The kind of world that produces anxiety is actually a world of relative safety, a world in which no one feels that he himself is facing sudden death. Possibly sudden death may strike a certain number of unidentified other people—but not him. The anxiety exists as an uneasy state of mind, in which one has a feeling that something unspecified and undeterminable may go wrong. If the world seems to be going well, this produces anxiety—for good times may end. If the world is going badly—it may get worse. Anxiety tends to be without locus; the anxious person doesn't know whether to blame himself or other people. He isn't sure whether it is the current year or the Administration or a change in climate or the atom bomb that is to blame for this undefined sense of unease.

It is clear that we have developed a society which depends on having the *right* amount of anxiety to make it work. Psychiatrists have been heard to say, "He didn't have enough anxiety to get well," indicating that, while we agree that too much anxiety is inimical to mental health, we have come to rely on anxiety to push and prod us into seeing a doctor about a symptom which may indicate cancer, into checking up on that old life-insurance policy which may have out-of-date clauses in it, into having a conference with Billy's teacher even though his report card looks all right.

People who are anxious enough keep their car insurance up, have the brakes checked, don't take a second drink when they have to drive, are careful where they go and with whom they drive on holidays. People who are too anxious either refuse to go into cars at all—and so complicate the ordinary course of life—or drive so tensely and overcautiously that they help cause accidents. People who aren't anxious enough take chance after chance, which increases the terrible death toll of the roads.

On balance, our age of anxiety represents a large advance over savage and peasant cultures. Out of a productive system of technology drawing upon enormous resources, we have created a nation in which anxiety has replaced terror and despair, for all except the severely disturbed. The specter of hunger means something only to those Americans who can identify themselves with the millions of hungry people on other continents. The specter of terror may still be roused in some by a knock at the door in a few parts of the South, or in those who have just escaped from a totalitarian regime or who have kin still behind the Curtains.

But in this twilight world which is neither at peace nor at war, and where there is insurance against certain immediate, downright, personal disasters, for most Americans there remains only anxiety over what may happen, might happen, could happen.

This is the world out of which grows the hope, for the first time in history, of a society where there will be freedom from want and freedom from fear. Our very anxiety is born of our knowledge of what is now possible for each and for all. The number of people who consult psychiatrists today is not, as is sometimes felt, a symptom of increasing mental ill health, but rather the precursor of a world in which the hope of genuine mental health will be open to everyone, a world in which no individual feels that he need be hopelessly brokenhearted, a failure, a menace to others or a traitor to himself.

But if, then, our anxieties are actually signs of hope, why is there such a voice of discontent abroad in the land? I think this comes perhaps because our anxiety exists without an accompanying recognition of the tragedy which will always be inherent in human life, however well we build our world. We many banish hunger, and fear of sorcery, violence or secret police; we may bring up children who have learned to trust life and who have the spontaneity and curiosity necessary to devise ways of making trips to the moon; we cannot—as we have tried to do—banish death itself.

Americans who stem from generations which left their old people behind and never closed their parents' eyelids in death, and who have experienced the additional distance from death provided by two world wars fought far from our shores are today pushing away from them both a recognition of death and a recognition of the tremendous significance—for the future—of the way we live our lives. Acceptance of the inevitability of death, which, when faced, can give dignity to life, and acceptance of our inescapable role in the modern world, might transmute our anxiety about making the right choices, taking the right precautions, and the right risks into the sterner stuff of responsibility, which ennobles the whole face rather than furrowing the forehead with the little anxious wrinkles of worry.

Worry in an empty context means that men die daily little deaths. But good anxiety—not about the things that were left undone long ago, but which return to haunt and harry men's minds, but active, vivid anxiety about what must be done and that quickly—binds men to life with an intense concern.

This is still a world in which too many of the wrong things happen somewhere. But this is a world in which we now have the means to make a great many more of the right things happen everywhere. For Americans, the generalization which a Swedish social scientist made about our attitudes on race relations is true in many other fields: anticipated change which we feel is right and necessary but difficult makes us unduly anxious and apprehensive, but such change, once consumated, brings a glow of relief. We are still a people who—in the literal sense—believe in making good.

Attaining
a Unique
Place

Eleanor Roosevelt: The Awakening

by Archibald MacLeish

Two men, a poet and a statesman, approach the life of a real woman of our times—one from the perspective of her childhood and the other from her death—and both capture the qualities of "the first lady" perhaps "of the world."

All human lives have contrast, conflict, drama: death and the inevitablity of death see to that. The difference is that, in the greater lives, the contrast is also greater. As it is in the life of Eleanor Roosevelt. It would be difficult to imagine a life with sharper contrast, a more dramatic disparity, between beginning and end. She dies the object of the world's attention and is buried not only with the ceremonies reserved for the great but with something even the greatest rarely achieve—the real grief of millions of human beings.

But she was born at the farthest possible remove from all this. Not in poverty and insignificance—the poor and the insignificant have been Lincoln before this. Not in poverty and insignificance but in banality—an almost inexpressible banality.

Nothing in history has been more banal than the provinciality of the life of the rich and well-born in Edith Wharton's New York, and Eleanor Roosevelt was born smack in the middle of it; the granddaughter of an incredible woman who still thought in 1917 that a "gentleman" was a man who hired somebody else to go to war for him; the daughter of a social "belle" and of a charming horseman and hunter who retired from living when he could no longer ride.

Furthermore, Eleanor Roosevelt, though she did not

"belong" to her mother's world, had no desire as a young girl *but* to belong to it. She suffered throughout her youth, because she was not the beauty her mother's family was supposed to produce, or because she lacked the graces young girls of her class were supposed to have, or because her grandmother, when her grandmother took over her life, didn't approve of her. Even years later, when she had acquired the kind of mother-in-law her particular world was capable of producing, she still spent her energies, wanting to be loved—wanting to belong to her class and place and time but failing even then.

And out of *that* comes *this*. Out of the rejected child of a peculiarly unpromising generation in the most provincial city of a provincial age—a New York in which rich men's daughters *were* actually married off to English dukes— comes the most remarkable woman of her century.

And comes how? Not in any readily explicable way. Not by education certainly, for she had next to no formal education—though what little she had played a part and an important part: the principal of her English school, for obvious example. But how then? By some delayed but understandable working of the genes? Theodore Roosevelt coming out in a niece whose Roosevelt father was apparently innocent of anything but an extraordinary charm— a gift for animals and children and a noticeable warmth of heart? It is possible, but the genes usually make themselves felt from the beginning and there is little in Eleanor Roosevelt as a girl or even as a young woman to recall the zest and bounce and combativeness of T. R.

Was it then the shock of her husband's illness? No. Her husband's illness forced her to assert herself against her mother-in-law, but the self she asserted was already there —had, indeed, been there for some time: She had begun to discover resources of power and feeling in herself as far back as her first Washington years when she learned that she could run her house and her hospital work and her tasks as the wife of the Assistant Secretary of the Navy and still wake up mornings with strength enough left to do it all over again day after day after day.

My own notion is that the answer may perhaps be found in the old human wisdom which expresses itself in myths like the myth of the sleeping beauty. People aren't "made" by themselves or by anyone else. They are released to *be* what they always were but had never known they were. And what releases them is the touch of life— the "kiss" of life, the fairy tale would say. For thirty years and more, the woman who was to change the world lay in a sound, if not too comfortable, sleep back of the thorns and thickets of the decaying castle of the dying age into which she was born.

But though that dream of waking petered out, *she*— she *herself*—was still there. And the time came when she knew that she was there—knew what she really was. We can name that time, I think. It was during the First World War—that most terrible of all wars when human misery and human suffering were revealed with a candor and brutality never equaled until then. It was at the moment when she realized that there was something she, Eleanor Roosevelt, could *do* about that misery and that suffering. I don't know—I can't be certain now—but I think we will find that this moment came to her—this burning sense of human need, of human suffering, which is to say of human life—when she first saw, in St. Elizabeth's Hospital in Washington, the shell-shocked sailors and Marines who had been sent back to the primitive care then available, and first realized that if something was to be done about inexpressible unhappiness, she—she herself—would have to do it.

If this is true, then the rest of her life was the playing out of that tremendous discovery—a discovery which had to wait for scope and opportunity until her husband's illness forced her into politics to keep *him* there and eventually led her to what we must call, I suppose, her career. But if this, or something like it, is true, then the dark and light of this portrait of ours will be found in the contrast, the unlikely, the almost incredible, contrast, between the long sleep in the impenetrable castle and the freedom and passion of the awakened woman.

And the drama of the portrait will be achieved in the discovery of the real woman behind the sleeping mask: the extraordinary paradox of the little girl who agreed with everyone in order to be loved and the awakened woman who said what she thought even when, as in her protest against the Japanese concentration camps in California at the beginning of the Second World War, it brought a whole sky of public disapprobation down on her head.

Her Journeys
Are Over

by Adlai E. Stevenson

One week ago this afternoon, in the Rose Garden at Hyde Park, Eleanor Roosevelt came home for the last time. Her journeys are over. The remembrance now begins.

In gathering here to honor her, we engage in a self-serving act. It is we who are trying, by this ceremony of tribute, to deny the fact that we have lost her, and, at least, to prolong the farewell, and—possibly—to say some of the things we dared not say in her presence, because she would have turned aside such testimonial with impatience and gently asked us to get on with some of the more serious business of the meeting.

A grief perhaps not equaled since the death of her husband seventeen years ago is the world's best tribute to one of the great figures of our age—a woman whose lucid and luminous faith testified always for sanity in an insane time and for hope in a time of obscure hope—a woman who spoke for the good toward which man aspires in a world which has seen too much of the evil of which man is capable.

She lived seventy-eight years, most of the time in tireless activity as if she knew that only a frail fragment of the things that cry out to be done could be done in the lifetime of even the most fortunate. One has the melancholy sense that when she knew death was at hand, she was contemplating not what she achieved, but what she had not quite managed to do. And I know she wanted to go—when there was no more strength to do.

Yet how much she had done—how much still unchronicled! We dare not try to tabulate the lives she salvaged, the battles—known and unrecorded—she fought, the afflicted she comforted, the hovels she brightened, the faces and places, near and far, that were given some new radiance, some sound of music, by her endeavors. What other single human being has touched and transformed the existence of so many others? What better measure is there of the impact of anyone's life?

There was no sick soul too wounded to engage her mercy. There was no signal of human distress which she did not view as a personal summons. There was no affront to human dignity from which she fled because the timid cried "danger." And the number of occasions on which her intervention turned despair into victory we may never know.

Her life was crowded, restless, fearless. Perhaps she pitied most not those whom she aided in the struggle, but the more fortunate who were preoccupied with themselves and cursed with the self-deceptions of private success. She walked in the slums and ghettos of the world, not on a tour of inspection, nor as a condescending patron, but as one who could not feel complacent while others were hungry, and who could not find contentment while others were in distress. This was not sacrifice; this, for Mrs. Roosevelt, was the only meaningful way of life.

These were not conventional missions of mercy. What rendered this unforgettable woman so extraordinary was not merely her response to suffering; it was her comprehension of the complexity of the human condition. Not long before she died, she wrote that "within all of us there are two sides. One reaches for the stars, the other descends to the level of beasts." It was, I think, this discernment that made her so unfailingly tolerant of friends who faltered, and led her so often to remind the smug and the complacent that "there but for the grace of God. . . ."

But we dare not regard her as just a benign incarnation of good works. For she was not only a great woman and a great humanitarian, but a great democrat. I use the word with a small "d"—though it was, of course, equally true that she was a great Democrat with a capital "D." When I say that she was a great small "d" democrat, I mean that she had a lively and astute understanding of the nature of the democratic process. She was a master political strategist with a fine sense of humor. And, as she said, she loved a good fight.

She was a realist. Her compassion did not become sentimentality. She understood that progress was a long labor

of compromise. She mistrusted absolutism in all its forms—
the absolutism of the word and even more the absolutism
of the deed. She never supposed that all the problems of
life could be cured in a day or a year or a lifetime. Her
pungent and salty understanding of human behavior kept
her always in intimate contact with reality. I think this
was a primary source of her strength, because she never
thought that the loss of a battle meant the loss of a war,
nor did she suppose that a compromise which produced
only part of the objective sought was an act of corruption
or of treachery. She knew that no formula of words, no
combination of deeds, could abolish the troubles of life
overnight and usher in the millennium.

The miracle, I have tried to suggest, is how much tangible good she really did; how much realism and reason
were mingled with her instinctive compassion; how her
contempt for the perquisites of power ultimately won her
the esteem of so many of the powerful; and how, at her
death, there was a universality of grief that transcended
all the harsh boundaries of political, racial and religious
strife and, for a moment at least, united men in a vision of
what their world might be.

We do not claim the right to enshrine another mortal,
and this least of all would Mrs. Roosevelt have desired.
She would have wanted it said, I believe, that she well
knew the pressures of pride and vanity, the sting of bit-
terness and defeat, the gray days of national peril and
personal anguish. But she clung to the confident expectation that men could fashion their own tomorrows if they
could only learn that yesterday can be neither relived
nor revised.

Many who have spoken of her in these last few days
have used a word to which we all assent, because it speaks
a part of what we feel. They have called her "a lady," a
"great lady," "the first lady of the world." But the word
"lady," though it says much about Eleanor Roosevelt, does
not say all. To be incapable of self-concern is not a
negative virtue; it is the other side of a coin that has a
positive face—the most positive, I think, of all the faces.
And to enhance the humanity of others is not a kind
of humility; it is a kind of pride—the noblest of all the
forms of pride. No man or woman can respect other men

and women who does not respect life. And to respect life is to love it. Eleanor Roosevelt loved life—and that, perhaps, is the most meaningful thing that can be said about her, for it says so much beside.

It takes courage to love life. Loving it demands imagination and perception and the kind of patience women are more apt to have than men—the bravest and most understanding women. And loving it takes something more beside—it takes a gift for life, a gift for love.

Eleanor Roosevelt's childhood was unhappy—miserably unhappy, she sometimes said. But it was Eleanor Roosevelt who also said that "one must never, for whatever reason, turn his back on life." She did not mean that duty should compel us. She meant that life should. "Life," she said, "was meant to be lived." A simple statement. An obvious statement. But a statement that by its obviousness and its simplicity challenges the most intricate of all the philosophies of despair.

Many of the admonitions she bequeathed us are neither new thoughts nor novel concepts. Her ideas were, in many respects, old-fashioned—as old as the Sermon on the Mount, as the reminder that it is more blessed to give than to receive. In the words of St. Francis that she loved so well: "For it is in the giving that we receive."

She imparted to the familiar language—nay, what too many have come to treat as the clichés—of Christianity a new poignancy and vibrance. She did so not by reciting them, but by proving that it is possible to live them. It is this above all that rendered her unique in her century. It was said of her contemptuously at times that she was a do-gooder, a charge leveled with similar derision against another public figure 1,962 years ago.

We who are assembled here are of various religious and political faiths, and perhaps different conceptions of man's destiny in the universe. It is not an irreverence, I trust, to say that the immortality Mrs. Roosevelt would have valued most would be found in the deeds and visions her life inspired in others, and in the proof that they would be faithful to the spirit of any tribute conducted in her name.

And now one can almost hear Mrs. Roosevelt saying that the speaker has already talked too long. So we must

say farewell. We are always saying farewell in this world
—always standing at the edge of loss attempting to retrieve some memory, some human meaning, from the
silence—something which was precious and is gone.

Often, although we know the absence well enough, we
cannot name it or describe it even. What left the world
when Lincoln died? Speaker after speaker in those aching
days tried to tell his family or his neighbors or his congregation. But no one found the words, not even Whitman.
"When lilacs last in the dooryard bloomed" can break
the heart, but not with Lincoln's greatness, only with his
loss. What the words could never capture was the man
himself. His deeds were known; every school child knew
them. But it was not his deeds the country mourned: it
was the man—the mastery of life which made the greatness of the man.

It is always so. On that April day when Franklin
Roosevelt died, it was not a President we wept for. It
was a man. In Archibald MacLeish's words:

Fagged out, worn down, sick
With the weight of his own bones, the task finished,
The war won, the victory assured,
The glory left behind him for the others,
(And the wheels roll up through
      the night in the sweet land
In the cool air in the spring
      between the lanterns).

It is so now. What we have lost in Eleanor Roosevelt
is not her life. She lived that out to the full. What we
have lost, what we wish to recall for ourselves, to remember, is what she was herself. And who can name it?
But she left "a name to shine on the entablatures of truth,
forever."

We pray that she has found peace, and a glimpse of
sunset. But today we weep for ourselves. We are lonelier;
someone has gone from one's own life—who was like
the certainty of refuge; and someone has gone from the
world—who was like a certainty of honor.

The Harvard Man Who Put the Ease in Casey's Manner

by Martin Gardner

A writer uncovers the life story of the forgotten man who wrote the one poem every boy remembers.

A sly way to start an argument in a saloon is to quote "Casey at the Bat." It is so well known that hardly anyone knows it—but almost everyone, especially in saloons along toward closing time, is convinced he does. Not the whole thing, maybe, but certainly enough to lay down the law about it. If you really know the poem, and have paced your drinks wisely, you can win any number of bets. What was the score, for instance, when Casey came to bat? ("The score stood four to two with but one inning more to play.") What players were on base and how did they get there? (Look it up, why don't you?) Who—and this is the one to rock the boilermaker literati back on their barstools—who wrote "Casey at the Bat?"

The name may be on the tip of everyone's tongue but it's nice to be the one to blurt it out. The author of "Casey" was Ernest Lawrence Thayer, son of Edward Davis Thayer, a wealthy New England textile manufacturer. Ernest was born in Lawrence, Mass. on August 14, 1863. By the time he entered Harvard the family had moved to Worcester, where the elder Thayer ran one of his several woolen mills. At Harvard young Thayer made a brilliant record as a major in philosophy. The great William James was his teacher and friend. Thayer belonged to the Hasty Pudding Club. He was a member of the exclusive Fly Club and Delta Kappa Epsilon fraternity. He edited the college's humor magazine, the Harvard *Lampoon*. His best friend, Samuel E. Winslow (later a Congressman from Massachusetts), was captain of the senior baseball team. During his last year at Harvard, Thayer never missed a ball game.

Another friend of Thayer's college years was the business manager of the *Lampoon,* William Randolph Hearst. In 1885, when Thayer was graduated *magna cum laude*—he was Phi Beta Kappa and the Ivy orator of his class—Hearst was unceremoniously booted out of Harvard Yard. (He had a habit of playing practical jokes that no one in the faculty thought funny; for example, sending chamber pots to professors, their names inscribed thereon.) Hearst's father had recently bought the ailing *San Francisco Examiner.* Now that young Will was in want of something to occupy his time, the elder Hearst turned the paper over to him.

Thayer, in the meantime, after wandering around Europe with no particular goal, had settled in Paris to brush up on his French. Would he consider, Hearst cabled him, returning to the U.S. to write a humor column for the *Examiner's* Sunday supplement? To the great annoyance of his father, who expected him to take over American Woolen Mills someday, Thayer agreed.

Thayer's Sunday column, under the by-line of "Phin" (at Harvard his friends had called him Phinney), began in 1886. Every other Sunday he tossed into the column a comic ballad that he dashed off in a few hours. These ballads started in the fall of 1887 and continued for several months. Then ill health forced Thayer to return to Worcester. For a while he continued sending ballads to the *Examiner.* The last of them was "Casey." It ran on June 3, 1888, page 4, column 4, sandwiched between editorials on the left and a weekly column by Ambrose Bierce on the right.

No one paid much attention to the poem. Baseball fans in San Francisco chuckled over it and a few eastern papers reprinted it, but it probably would have been quickly forgotten had it not been for a sequence of improbable events. In New York City, a young comedian and bass singer, DeWolf Hopper, was appearing in a comic opera at Wallack's theater. One evening (the exact date is a matter of controversy; it was probably late in 1888 or sometime in 1889) the New York Giants and the Chicago White Stockings were invited to the show as guests of the management. What could he do on stage, Hopper asked himself, for the special benefit of these men? I have just the thing, said Archibald Clavering Gunter, a novelist and friend. He took from his pocket a ragged newspaper clipping that he had cut from the *Examiner* on a recent trip to San Francisco. It was "Casey."

This poem, insisted Gunter, is great. Why not memorize it and deliver it on the stage? Hopper recited it in the middle of the second act, with the Giants in boxes on one side of the theater, the White Stockings in boxes on the other.

Hopper made the recitation a permanent part of his repertoire. It became his most famous bit. Wherever he went, whatever the show in which he was appearing, there were always curtain shouts for "Casey." By his own count, he recited it more than 10,000 times, experimenting with hundreds of slight variations in emphasis and gesture to keep his mind from wandering. It took him exactly five minutes and forty seconds to deliver the poem.

All over the U.S. newspapers and magazines began to reprint it. No one knew who Phin was. Editors either dropped the name altogether or substituted their own or a fictitious one. Stanzas were lost. Lines got botched by printers or rewritten by editors who fancied themselves able to improve the original. Scarcely two printings of the poem were the same. In one early reprinting (by *The Sporting Times,* July 29, 1888) Mudville was changed to Boston and Casey's name to Kelly in honor of Mike (King) Kelly, a famous Boston star, about whom the popular song "Slide, Kelly, Slide" had been written.

From time to time various Caseys who played baseball in the late 1800's claimed to have been the inspiration for the ballad, but Thayer emphatically denied that he had had any ballplayer in mind for any of the men mentioned in his ballad. When the *Syracuse Post-Standard* wrote to ask him about this, he replied with a letter that is reprinted in full in Lee Allen's entertaining book on baseball, *The Hot Stove League* (1955):

> The verses owe their existence to my enthusiasm for college baseball, not as a player, but as a fan [Thayer wrote]. The poem has no basis in fact. The only Casey actually involved, I am sure about him, was not a ballplayer. He was a big, dour Irish lad

of my high school days. While in high school, I
composed and printed myself a very tiny sheet, less
than two inches by three. In one issue, I ventured
to gag, as we say, this Casey boy. He didn't like it
and he told me so, and, as he discoursed, his big,
clenched, red hands were white at the knuckles.
This Casey's name never again appeared in the
Monohippic Gazette. But I suspect the incident,
many years after, suggested the title for the poem.
It was a taunt thrown to the winds. God grant he
never catches me.

By 1900 almost everyone in America knew the poem
but hardly anyone knew who wrote it. Hopper himself did
not discover the author's identity until about five years after
he began reciting it. One evening, having delivered the
poem in a Worcester theater, he received a note inviting
him to a local club to meet "Casey's" author. "Over the
details of wassail that followed," Hopper wrote later, "I
will draw a veil of charity." He did disclose, however,
that the club members had persuaded Thayer himself to
stand up and recite "Casey." It was, Hopper declared, the
worst delivery of the poem he had ever heard. "In a sweet
dulcet whisper he [Thayer] implored Casey to murder the
umpire, and gave this cry of animal rage all the emphasis
of a caterpillar."

Thayer remained in Worcester for many years, doing
his best to please his father by managing one of the family
mills. He kept quietly to himself, studying philosophy in
his spare hours and reading classical literature, a gracious,
charming, modest man, soft-spoken, slight of build, a bit
hard of hearing and with only the lowest opinion of his
own verse. He dashed off a few more comic ballads in
1896, for Hearst's *New York Journal,* but he never considered them worth collecting in a book.

During my brief acquaintance with the *Examiner,*
[Thayer once wrote] I put out large quantities of
nonsense, both prose and verse, sounding the whole
newspaper gamut from advertisements to editorials.
In general quality "Casey" (at least to my judgment) is neither better nor worse than much of the

other stuff. Its persistent vogue is simply unaccountable, and it would be hard to say, all things considered, if it has given me more pleasure than annoyance. The constant wrangling about authorship, from which I have tried to keep aloof, has certainly filled me with disgust.

Throughout his life he refused to discuss payments for reprintings of "Casey." "All I ask is never to be reminded of it again," he told one publisher. "Make it anything you wish."

Never happy in the family mills, Thayer finally quit working for them altogether. After a few years of travel abroad he retired in 1912 to Santa Barbara, Calif. The following year—he was then fifty—he married Mrs. Rosalind Buel Hammett, a widow from St. Louis. They had no children.

Thayer remained in Santa Barbara until his death in 1940.

"Casey" has had many imitations, sequels and parodies. Two silent motion pictures were based on Thayer's poem. The first, in 1916, starred Hopper himself as the mighty Casey. Thayer is said to have refused to appear in a short introductory scene. A second *Casey at the Bat* was released in 1927, with Wallace Beery in the leading role. (I can still recall Beery, bat in one hand and beer mug in the other, whacking the ball so hard that an outfielder has to mount a horse to retrieve it.) More recently, an animated short by Walt Disney featured the voice of Jerry Colonna reciting the ballad.

Several flimsy paperback editions of the poem, with illustrations, came out around the turn of the century. A. C. McClurg published a more substantial edition in 1912 with pictures by Dan Sayre Groesbeck. In 1964 Prentice-Hall brought out a hard-cover "Casey," profusely illustrated by Paul Frame; that same year Franklin Watts issued another, with art by Leonard Everett Fisher and a short introduction by Casey Stengel. The poem has also been illustrated innumerable times for newspaper and magazine appearances. The variant readings—including revisions by Thayer himself—might well make a thesis for a graduate student desperate for a subject.

How can one explain "Casey's" undying popularity? It is not great poetry. It was written carelessly. Parts of it are certainly doggerel. Yet it is almost impossible to read it several times without memorizing whole chunks, and there are lines so perfectly expressed, given the poem's intent, that one cannot imagine a word changed for the better. The late T. S. Eliot admired the ballad so much that he even wrote a parody about a cat, "Growl-tiger's Last Stand," in which many of Thayer's lines are echoed.

The poem's secret can be found, of all places, in the autobiography of George Santayana, another famous Harvard philosopher. Santayana was one of Thayer's associate editors on the *Lampoon*. "The man who gave the tone to the *Lampoon* at that time," Santayana writes, "was Ernest Thayer. . . . He seemed a man apart, his wit was not so much jocular as Mercutio-like, curious and whimsical, as if he saw the broken edges of things that appear whole. There was some obscurity in his play with words, and a feeling (which I shared) that the absurd side of things is pathetic. Probably nothing in his later performance may bear out what I have just said of him, because American life was then becoming unfavorable to idiosyncrasies of any sort, and the current smoothed and rounded out all the odd pebbles."

But Santayana was wrong. One thing *did* bear this out, and that was "Casey." It is precisely the blend of absurd and tragic that lies at the heart of Thayer's poem. Casey is the giant of baseball who, at his moment of greatest possible triumph, strikes out. A pathetic figure, yet comic because of the supreme arrogance and confidence with which he approached the plate: "There was ease in Casey's manner." It is the shock of contrast between the enormous buildup and the final fizzle that produces the poem's explosion point. The story of Casey has become an American myth because Casey is the incomparable symbol of the great and glorious poop-out.

One might argue that Thayer, with his extraordinary beginning at Harvard, his friendship with James and Santayana, his lifelong immersion in philosophy and the great books, was himself something of a Casey. In later years his friends were constantly urging him to write, but he would always shake his head and reply, "I have nothing to say." Not until just before his death, at the age of seventy-seven, did he make an attempt to put some serious thoughts on paper. By then it was too late. *"Now* I have something to say," he said, "and I am too weak to say it."

But posterity's judgments are hard to anticipate. Thayer's writing career was no strikeout. He swatted one magnificent, eternal home run—"Casey"—and as long as baseball is played on this old earth, on Mudville, the air will be shattered over and over again by the force of Casey's blow.

Casey at the Bat

It looked extremely rocky for the Mudville nine that day;
The score stood two to four, with but one inning left to play.
So, when Cooney died at second, and Burrows did the same,
A pallor wreathed the features of the patrons of the game.

A straggling few got up to go, leaving there the rest,
With that hope which springs eternal within the human
    breast.
For they thought: "If only Casey could get a whack at
    that,"
They'd put even money now, with Casey at the bat.

But Flynn preceded Casey, and likewise so did Blake,
And the former was a pudd'n, and the latter was a fake.
So on that stricken multitude a deathlike silence sat;
For there seemed but little chance of Casey's getting to
    the bat.

But Flynn let drive a "single," to the wonderment of all.
And the much-despisèd Blakey "tore the cover off the ball."
And when the dust had lifted, and they saw what had
    occurred,
There was Blakey safe at second, and Flynn a-huggin' third.

Then from the gladdened multitude went up a joyous yell—
It rumbled in the mountaintops, it rattled in the dell;
It struck upon the hillside and rebounded on the flat;
For Casey, mighty Casey, was advancing to the bat.

There was ease in Casey's manner as he stepped into his
    place,
There was pride in Casey's bearing and a smile on Casey's
    face;
And when responding to the cheers he lightly doffed his hat,
No stranger in the crowd could doubt 'twas Casey at the bat.

Ten thousand eyes were on him as he rubbed his hands
    with dirt.
Five thousand tongues applauded when he wiped them on his
    shirt;
Then when the writhing pitcher ground the ball into his hip,
Defiance glanced in Casey's eye, a sneer curled Casey's lip.

And now the leather-covered sphere came hurtling through
    the air,
And Casey stood a-watching it in haughty grandeur there.
Close by the sturdy batsman the ball unheeded sped;
"That ain't my style," said Casey. "Strike one," the
    umpire said.

From the benches, black with people, there went up a
    muffled roar,
Like the beating of the storm waves on the stern and distant
    shore.
"Kill him! kill the umpire!" shouted someone on the stand;
And it's likely they'd have killed him had not Casey raised
    his hand.

With a smile of Christian charity great Casey's visage shone;
He stilled the rising tumult, he made the game go on;
He signaled to the pitcher, and once more the spheroid flew;
But Casey still ignored it, and the umpire said, "Strike two."

"Fraud!" cried the maddened thousands, and the echo
    answered "Fraud!"
But one scornful look from Casey and the audience was
    awed;
They saw his face grow stern and cold, they saw his muscles
    strain,
And they knew that Casey wouldn't let the ball go by
    again.

The sneer is gone from Casey's lips, his teeth are clenched in hate,
He pounds with cruel vengeance his bat upon the plate;
And now the pitcher holds the ball, and now he lets it go,
And now the air is shattered by the force of Casey's blow.

Oh, somewhere in this favored land the sun is shining bright,
The band is playing somewhere, and somewhere hearts are light;
And somewhere men are laughing, and somewhere children shout,
But there is no joy in Mudville—Mighty Casey has struck out!

—ERNEST LAWRENCE THAYER

The Monster

by Deems Taylor

*A music critic—composer balances the shocking personal
qualities of a man against the unique contributions of
his musical gift.*

He was an undersized little man, with a head too big
for his body—a sickly little man. His nerves were bad. He
had skin trouble. It was agony for him to wear anything
next to his skin coarser than silk. And he had delusions of
grandeur.

He was a monster of conceit. Never for one minute did
he look at the world or at people, except in relation to himself. He was not only the most important person in the
world, to himself; in his own eyes he was the only person
who existed. He believed himself to be one of the greatest
dramatists in the world, one of the greatest thinkers, and
one of the greatest composers. To hear him talk he was
Shakespeare, and Beethoven, and Plato, rolled into one.
And you would have had no difficulty in hearing him talk.
He was one of the most exhausting conversationalists that
ever lived. An evening with him was an evening spent in
listening to a monologue. Sometimes he was brilliant;
sometimes he was maddeningly tiresome. But whether he
was being brilliant or dull, he had one sole topic of conversation: himself. What *he* thought and what *he* did.

He had a mania for being in the right. The slightest hint
of disagreement, from anyone, on the most trivial point,
was enough to set him off on a harangue that might last
for hours, in which he proved himself right in so many
ways, and with such exhausting volubility, that in the end
his hearer, stunned and deafened, would agree with him,
for the sake of peace.

It never occurred to him that he and his doing were not

of the most intense and fascinating interest to anyone with whom he came in contact. He had theories about almost any subject under the sun, including vegetarianism, the drama, politics, and music; and in support of these theories he wrote pamphlets, letters, books . . . thousands upon thousands of words, hundreds and hundreds of pages. He not only wrote these things, and published them—usually at somebody else's expense—but he would sit and read them aloud, for hours, to his friends and his family.

He wrote operas; and no sooner did he have the synopsis of a story, but he would invite—or rather summon—a crowd of his friends to his house and read it aloud to them. Not for criticism. For applause. When the complete poem was written, the friends had to come again, and hear *that* read aloud. Then he would publish the poem, sometimes years before the music that went with it was written. He played the piano like a composer, in the worst sense of what that implies, and he would sit down at the piano before parties that included some of the finest pianists of his time, and play for them, by the hour, his own music, needless to say. He had a composer's voice. And he would invite eminent vocalists to his house, and sing them his operas, taking all the parts.

He had the emotional stability of a six-year-old child. When he felt out of sorts, he would rave and stamp, or sink into suicidal gloom and talk darkly of going to the East to end his days as a Buddhist monk. Ten minutes later, when something pleased him, he would rush out of doors and run around the garden, or jump up and down on the sofa, or stand on his head. He could be grief-stricken over the death of a pet dog, and he could be callous and heartless to a degree that would have made a Roman emperor shudder.

He was almost innocent of any sense of responsibility. Not only did he seem incapable of supporting himself, but it never occurred to him that he was under any obligation to do so. He was convinced that the world owed him a living. In support of this belief, he borrowed money from everybody who was good for a loan—men, women, friends, or strangers. He wrote begging letters by the score, sometimes groveling without shame, at others loftily offering his intended benefactor the privilege of contributing to his

support, and being mortally offended if the recipient de-
clined the honor. I have found no record of his ever paying or repaying money to anyone who did not have a legal
claim upon it.

What money he could lay his hands on he spent like an
Indian rajah. The mere prospect of a performance of one
of his operas was enough to set him running up bills amount-
ing to ten times the amount of his prospective royalties. On
an income that would reduce a more scrupulous man to
doing his own laundry, he would keep two servants. Without enough money in his pocket to pay his rent, he would
have the walls and ceiling of his study lined with pink silk.
No one will ever know—certainly he never knew—how
much money he owed. We do know that his greatest benefactor gave him 6,000 dollars to pay the most pressing of
his debts in one city, and a year later had to give him
16,000 dollars to enable him to live in another city without being thrown into jail for debt.

He was equally unscrupulous in other ways. An endless
procession of women marches through his life. His first wife
spent twenty years enduring and forgiving his infidelities.
His second wife had been the wife of his most devoted
friend and admirer, from whom he stole her. And even
while he was trying to persuade her to leave her first husband he was writing to a friend to inquire whether he could
suggest some wealthy woman—*any* wealthy woman—whom
he could marry for her money.

He was completely selfish in his other personal relationships. His liking for his friends was measured solely by the
completeness of their devotion to him, or by their usefulness to him, whether financial or artistic. The minute they
failed him—even by so much as refusing a dinner invita-
tion—or began to lessen in usefulness, he cast them off
without a second thought. At the end of his life he had
exactly one friend left whom he had known even in
middle age.

He had a genius for making enemies. He would insult a
man who disagreed with him about the weather. He would
pull endless wires in order to meet some man who admired
his work, and was able and anxious to be of use to him—
and would proceed to make a mortal enemy of him with
some idiotic and wholly uncalled-for exhibition of arro-

gance and bad manners. A character in one of his operas
was a caricature of one of the most powerful music
critics of his day. Not content with burlesquing him, he
invited the critic to his house and read him the libretto
aloud in front of his friends.

The name of this monster was Richard Wagner. Everything that I have said about him you can find on record—
in newspapers, in police reports, in the testimony of people
who knew him, in his own letters, between the lines of
his autobiography. And the curious thing about this record
is that it doesn't matter in the least.

Because this undersized, sickly, disagreeable, fascinating
little man was right all the time. The joke was on us. He
was one of the world's great dramatists; he *was* a great
thinker; he *was* one of the most stupendous musical geniuses
that, up to now, the world has ever seen. The world did
owe him a living. People couldn't know those things at the
time, I suppose; and yet to us, who know his music, it
does seem as though they should have known. What if he
did talk about himself all the time? If he talked about himself for twenty-four hours every day for the span of his
life he would not have uttered half the number of words
that other men have spoken and written about him since his
death.

When you consider what he wrote—thirteen operas and
music dramas, eleven of them still holding the stage, eight
of them unquestionably worth ranking among the world's
great musico-dramatic masterpieces—when you listen to
what he wrote, the debts and heartaches that people had to
endure from him don't seem much of a price. Eduard Hans-
lick, the critic whom he caricatured in *Die Meistersinger*
and who hated him ever after, now lives only because he
was caricatured in *Die Meistersinger*. The women whose
hearts he broke are long since dead; and the man who
could never love anyone but himself has made them death-
less atonement, I think, with *Tristan und Isolde*. Think of
the luxury with which for a time, at least, fate rewarded
Napoleon, the man who ruined France and looted Europe;
and then perhaps you will agree that a few thousand dollars' worth of debts were not too heavy a price to pay for
the *Ring* trilogy.

What if he was faithless to his friends and to his wives?

He had one mistress to whom he was faithful to the day of his death: music. Not for a single moment did he ever compromise with what he believed, with what he dreamed. There is not a line of his music that could have been conceived by a little mind. Even when he is dull, or downright bad, he is dull in the grand manner. There is a greatness about his worst mistakes. Listening to his music, one does not forgive him for what he may or may not have been. It is not a matter of forgiveness. It is a matter of being dumb with wonder that his poor brain and body didn't burst under the torment of the demon of creative energy that lived inside him, struggling, clawing, scratching to be released; tearing, shrieking at him to write the music that was in him. The miracle is that what he did in the little space of seventy years could have been done at all, even by a great genius. Is it any wonder that he had no time to be a man?

My Uncle Koppel
and Free Enterprise

by Harry Golden

An editor-writer-humorist traces the financial rise of his immigrant uncle and discovers a man greater than his career.

My uncle Koppel (K. Berger) was twenty years old when he came to America. The day after his arrival he opened a small butcher shop on Scammel Street, on New York's Lower East Side. For the next three years he opened up his shop at six o'clock in the morning, worked till after dark, cooked his meals on a stove in the back of the store, and pushed the meat block up against the front door to sleep. What English he learned he picked up from the truck drivers, who delivered the meat and the poultry. There was nothing unusual about this. There were thousands of immigrants who lived, worked, and died within the confines of a few city blocks. But with Koppel Berger it was to be different, because Uncle Koppel had imagination, courage, ability, and, above all, he seemed to know what America was all about.

It was 1904 and all America was singing, "Meet me in St. Louey, Louey, meet me at the Fair . . ." and my immigrant Uncle took the lyrics literally. He arrived in St. Louis, Missouri, with five hundred dollars, a wife, and a vocabulary of about thirty words of broken English. He acquired a lease on a rooming house, which accommodated thirty guests. Again he worked night and day. His wife did the laundry, cleaned the rooms, and made the beds; Uncle Koppel carried the baggage, roomed the guests, kept the accounts, carried the coal, made the hot water, and told his guests that he was an employee so that he could also run all their errands. The St. Louis Fair was a success, and so was Koppel Berger. After two years, he and his wife and infant son returned to New York with a little over eight thousand dollars.

Up on Broadway at 38th Street was the old Hotel Normandie, which was not doing so well under the management of the great prize fighter, the original Kid McCoy (Norman Selby).

With a vocabulary of about seventy-five words of broken English, Uncle Koppel took over the lease on this 250-room hotel in the heart of the theatrical district. Of course, even a genius must have some luck, too, and we must concede that Koppel Berger acquired the Hotel Normandie at exactly the right moment. New York and America were becoming "hotel-minded"; in addition, the theatre was entering upon its greatest era, a "golden age" such as we shall never see again. Between 1907 and 1927, there were literally hundreds and hundreds of road shows and stock companies; burlesque was in all its glory; dozens of opera "extravaganzas" were playing all over the country; vaudeville was at its all-time peak; and on Broadway itself, there were at least one hundred and fifty attractions produced each year.

In those days, "actors" and "actresses" were not particularly welcome at the best hotels. In fact, many New Yorkers will remember the signs on some small hotels and rooming houses, "Actors Accommodated."

In various stages of their careers, Uncle Koppel's Hotel Normandie was "home" to such players as Nat Wills, Wilton Lackaye, Cissie Loftus, Grant Mitchell, Lionel and John Barrymore, Otto Kruger, Doc Rockwell, W. C. Fields, Julian Eltinge, Tully Marshall, Tyrone Power, Sr., Dustin Farnum, Marie Cahill, and, of course, hundreds of lesser-known personalities. They had fun with Koppel Berger. They mimicked his accent; they made jokes of his hotel from the vaudeville stage; and they played tricks on the live fish he had swimming in a bathtub every Friday. Mike Jacobs, too, got started at the Hotel Normandie under Uncle Koppel. The man who later controlled the champion, Joe Louis, as well as the "prize-fight" business itself, started with a small ticket stand at the hotel, and the first time I ever saw Mike, he was sliding down the lobby bannister like a kid, with his brother Jake "catching" him. I used to

go to the Normandie once a week after school. My older
brother, Jack, was the night clerk, and my mother insisted
that he have a "Jewish" meal every Friday night, so I took
the Broadway streetcar to 38th Street, carrying a large
carton which included a pot of chicken soup, gefilte fish,
horseradish, boiled chicken, and "tsimmiss." My mother
had arranged with the chef at old Offer's Restaurant to let
me use his stove to get the stuff hot again. It was quite a
Friday afternoon, all around.

My brother, who later acquired some hotels of his own,
coined the phrase about "sleeping on the sign." A guest
came in and was told that the only room available would
cost $2.50. The guest said, "You've got $1.50 on the sign,"
and my brother told him, "Try and sleep on the sign."

Most of the one million dollars Uncle Koppel made in
the Hotel Normandie came during World War I, when he
put dozens of cots in the lobby and in the upstairs hall-
ways, to take care of the tremendous influx of job-seekers
and servicemen. The elevator in the Normandie was the old
cable variety, with the operator sitting in a swivel chair
and pulling the cable up and down.

*One night Uncle Koppel rented the swivel chair to a
guest who had to get a few hours' sleep.*

During this fabulous era of profits at the Normandie,
Uncle Koppel was acquiring other hotels—the old Calvert,
the Nassau, the Aberdeen, the Riviera in Newark; and,
finally, the famous old Martinique Hotel at the intersection
of Broadway and Sixth Avenue.

On the day that Koppel Berger took possession of the
Martinique, he stopped talking Yiddish. No one will ever
know why he stopped talking Yiddish, or how he expected
to get along on a vocabulary of about one hundred and fifty
words of broken English; but he saw it through to the
bitter end. My mother tried to trap him many times into
using a Yiddish word, but he never fell for the bait. Not
only did he stop talking Yiddish, but he no longer "understood" it.

My mother would say something to him and he'd look
at her with big innocent eyes and motion to one of us in
a helpless sort of way to act as an "interpreter." She would
become exasperated, call to him in Yiddish, and when she
turned to one of his "interpreters," she would rattle off a

string of "klulas" (Yiddish curse words), each of which
was a masterpiece; but old Koppel Berger did not move a
muscle or bat an eye. He simply smiled tolerantly, turned
to one of us children and asked, "Vot did she set?"

As you would expect, Uncle Koppel liquidated the
Hotel Normandie at the very "top." A year before the
crash, he sold the hotel to a fellow (a Mr. Lefcourt), who
couldn't wait to put up a forty-story building, but who met
the terrible depression before he reached the twenty-fifth
floor. In his last years, K. Berger retired to California, but
he never stopped making money. At the age of eighty-three,
he closed a deal for a large and profitable citrus business
on the Coast.

With it all, I believe Uncle Koppel was a sentimental man.
I remember while I was in high school, he once asked me
to do some "writing work" for him. He took me down to
the basement of the old Normandie Hotel where there
was a mountain of baggage left by guests who had not
paid the room rent in years past.

He wanted me to find the last known address of each,
for an advertisement, as provided by law, before he could
sell the stuff at auction. I looked over the vast number of
suitcases and trunks, and said, "Uncle Koppel, these actors
sure took away a lot of money from you."

Koppel Berger gently patted an old battered trunk with
a faded "Orpheum Circuit" imprint, and said, "These
actors *gave* me a lot of money."

Responding
to
Creative Experiences

Salt Crystals, Spider Webs, and Words

by Paul Engle

A poet and teacher of writing maintains that the precise difference between the many who want to record life and the few who can put their response to it in meaningful words lies in a distinction between self-expression and self-knowledge—the basis for the success of great writers.

Writing is like making love—it is astonishing how far pure instinct (if it really is pure) will carry you. It is also true of both these lyrical forms of expression that a few things consciously learned will push toward perfection what might otherwise be an ordinary act.

And yet—can writing actually be taught? Is there much more you can give to a beginner beyond Flaubert's no-nonsense advice of a kiss on the brow and a kick in the behind?

In pointing out that a writer crystallizes a concept, as when he endows a woman with qualities she simply does not have, Stendhal produced an image that, however little it flatters the ladies, does dramatize the process by which persuasive words can turn a dull object into something glittering and gay. He observes that a dead branch, dark and ugly, if left overnight in the salt mines of Salzburg, will be covered with crystals and next day will glitter in the sunlight.

This image of the salt crystals on the branch wisely and attractively illustrates what the writer does with that curious and secret substance called his "material." What writer has not been stopped by an eager-eyed and bushy-tailed person who cries out despairingly, "I've got the greatest material for a book, if I could just *write!*"

The first and most important point about writing is that

133

there is no such thing as material by itself, apart from the way in which a person sees it, feels toward it, and is able to give it organized form and expression in words. For a writer, form is a part of content, affecting it, realizing it. A man may go through the most dramatic and horrible experiences in war, but actually draw out of them less "material" for writing than shy Emily Dickinson in the second-floor room of an Amherst house, lowering notes in baskets out the window and thinking gently of death—or even (biographers speculate) of a man she knew but little, whom she might never see again.

Henry James said it first and beautifully when he wrote that experience is unlimited: "an immense sensibility, a kind of huge spider web of the finest silken threads suspended in the chamber of consciousness, and catching every air-borne particle in its tissue. It is the very atmosphere of the mind." This is crucial, for it is not what happens in the outside world that is of absolute significance, but what happens to that external event when it is discovered and then ordered by the internal power of a mind. James goes on to speak then of the creative aspect: "and when the mind is imaginative . . . it takes to itself the faintest hints of life, it converts the very pulse of the air into revelations."

By experience, then, a writer does not mean having adventures. In answering a critic who had complained about the novel that it is impossible to have one without bold action, James protested, "Why without adventure, more than without matrimony, or celibacy, or parturition, or cholera . . . ?"

Anything is suitable for fiction, which is not a record of incidents happening *to* men and women, but of the response they make within themselves to the incidents. This is because fiction deals with character, which determines action, and thus actions illustrate character. The conduct of a man in a ring fighting an enraged bull or the soft wave of a woman's hand are equally moving and suitable.

A thousand Frenchmen may walk down a Paris street and, turning a corner, forget the place. But Toulouse-Lautrec walking down the same street would see, with his shrewd eye, and remember, with his artist's force of retention, not bricks but visions. In this way the imagination works not only on the stuff that is stored in the mind, but also on the very act of experiencing. Like the pilot, the writer must see faster and more completely than the ordinary viewer of life.

Out of his practical skills in the writing of fiction, James described the process of the writer using his experience. "The power to guess the unseen from the seen," he said, "to trace the implication of things, to judge the whole piece by the pattern, the condition of feeling life in general so completely that you are well on your way to knowing any particular corner of it—this cluster of gifts may almost be said to constitute experience, and they occur in country and in town, and in the most differing stages of education. If experience consists of impressions, it may be said that impressions *are* experience, just as (have we not seen it?) they are the very air we breathe."

This is final wisdom about writing. The writer, when given an inch, takes an ell. Remember that an ell is forty-five inches. If that is the degree of heightening, then the eye of the writer must look at life with forty-five times as much perception. That is a marvelous degree of intensity, and in particular when it comes from the author of *Portrait of a Lady,* a book about which it has been remarked that, although it concerns the relationship between a man and a woman, there is only one kiss, and the heroine, poor thing, did not enjoy it.

But some will argue: writing, like all art, is intuitive, and any intrusion of the reason will destroy the lovely, natural thing. This is dead wrong. It reduces writing to the level of a child babbling without regard to the shape of what he is saying. It is, indeed, so much like the uninhibited confessions from the psychiatrist's couch, sodium amytal cheerfully flowing through the veins and breaking down shyness, that it would seem proper to give inhibition-removing drugs to the writer. He could sit there gaily listening to the rustlings of his unconscious. And of course the hallucinatory state would be the most creative of all.

It is quite possible that some good things could be thus spontaneously created. I met in India people who could induce visions. Yet surely the great and structured works of writing are done with the intelligence playing over against the intuition, each bracing the other, the mind giving form and sense, the intuition giving immediacy of impression, the stored-up memory, the deeply instinctive phrase.

To say that writing comes only from the intuition is to belittle it as coming from one narrow aspect of our lives alone. The opposite is true. The total life of the writer is the source of his work. All these go into his writing, in varying quantities: the senses, as of taste and touch, the rate of metabolism, the blood pressure, the digestion, the body temperature, the memory of things past, perhaps going back to the childhood not only of the writer but of the race itself, the liveliness and alertness of the brain, previous reading of books, shrewdness of insight into human character, the libido, the ear for the sound of language.

The writer, therefore, must not only have a more than ordinary capacity for life and the power to retain what he experiences in a readily available memory but he must also have an astonishing degree of self-knowledge. Unless he is aware of his material, he cannot use it, save for the always present quantity that flows up from the deep well of the unconscious recollection. Without access to knowledge of self, the writer can make dreams but not art. Dr. Lawrence S. Kubie says that without self-knowledge, "we can have the neurotic raw material of literature, but not mature literature. We can have no adults, but only aging children who are armed with words."

By self-knowledge I do not mean self-expression. Although all good writing always bears the individual mark, sound, and motion of the writer, he is not trying to put his own self into words, but to create a piece of writing. Often, the less of his own self involved or expressed, the better. His own personality ought to be dissolved into the images or characters of his book. The writer is offering us not reality, but his reaction to whatever reality he has experienced.

Yet the ego is important. It must be that within the creative person there is a constant tension beween an awareness of the reality around him, a thrusting up of the unconscious life and its memory, and the drive of the ego toward controlling these in a form that also heightens them. These are crude terms to describe subtle conditions, but the creation of any art is one of the most complex of human activities, involving every animal and human quality. The ego must shape the mortal impulses. It is here that something can indeed be taught about writing, for it is in this shaping that the individual's private events are turned into public forms. It is here that writing becomes an art and not merely a report on experience, and this is true of the best reporting.

How many boys have played around greenhouses? Swarms. But how many, on growing up, have put their feelings about that place into powerful poetry? Only Theodore Roethke. His account is proof.

Roethke asks what does it matter that he grew up in and around a beautiful greenhouse, hated school, worked in a pickle factory, lived sometimes quietly and sometimes foolishly and violently, and meant almost nothing to the people of his own state, the man in the street, but passionately desired their regard?

> All such details, and others like them [Roethke comments] seem particularly trivial and vulgar in my case because I have tried to put down in poems, as barely and honestly as possible, symbolically, what few nuggets of observation and, let us hope, spiritual wisdom I have managed to seize upon in the course of a conventional albeit sometimes disordered existence. I have tried to transmute and purify my "life," the sense of being defiled by it in both small and formal and somewhat blunt short poems, and latterly, in longer poems which try in their rhythms to catch the very movement of the mind itself, to trace the spiritual history of a protagonist (not "I" personally) of all haunted and harried men; to make in this series (now probably finished) a true and not arbitrary order which will permit many ranges of feeling, including humor. . . .

And then he says in verse:

> My heart sways with the world.
> I am that final thing,
> A man learning to sing.

Although this may suggest a self-consciousness not shared by all poets, it is further evidence of that deep need for self-knowledge that is a strength and a source. Roethke knew *what* he was trying to do in those moving and often tortured poems, and this awareness, far from inhibiting the imaginative freedom of the verse, enriched it. The cool mind, curiously enough, it seems, really can express a warm feeling.

Once the writer has a sense of his experience and of his own self, without illusion, and can be tough-minded about his own weakness and vulgarity, what else can he possibly learn? What can he *do* to make his writing better, assuming that he is not trapped in the conviction that writing is a wholly automatic outburst from underground?

He can examine the knowledge of their own writing habits great men have made available. It is odd the things writers have done. The German poet Schiller used to keep rotting apples under the lid of his desk because their smell helped him write. Pilots on the river at Rouen would see the light in Flaubert's study very late at night as he utterly shut himself away from the world to worry two pages of prose a week into the ruthlessly purified and perfected shape he demanded. Why this enormous care? The old wisecrack says that a physician who fails can always bury his patient out of sight. Frank Lloyd Wright remarked that an architect who fails can at least urge his client to plant vines. The writer, however, once his work is in print, can do nothing. There the text is, black on the page; any errors and ugliness will show forever. There are rare exceptions, of course, like William Butler Yeats, who, in his old age (with that marvelous lyrical mind hardened by the criticism of others), went back to the poems of his youth and cut out much of the sentimentality and soft, vague language.

Reticent as always, William Faulkner said that the tools of the writer's trade are paper, tobacco, food, and whiskey. Of these, the most dangerous is not tobacco or whiskey (writers are famous for abusing them), but paper. One of the most terrifying sights is that waiting, threatening blank sheet. Its force is proved by the Japanese writer who, after much success, could not, for a long time, push ahead with his writing. One autumn—and this is a true story—he disappeared. The next spring his body was found, after the snow had melted, high up in the mountains. Pinned to his jacket was a note only the suffering writer could have written: "I have done this because I could no longer endure the sight of the empty page."

All those writers who have commented on their craft agree that a work of art is work. How could the joining of passion and idea in slippery words be anything but a labor? That first really modern novel, *Madame Bovary*, was composed by Gustave Flaubert with the deliberation of a medieval monk illuminating a manuscript. The French novelist could write quickly and fluently, as his early books and his lively letters show, but he would never give up a sentence until it was beyond improving. To get his description of the landscape correct, he sat all day on a balcony looking through pieces of different-colored glass in order to note the changes in shape of fields and roads and trees hour by hour.

Never was a writer more emotionally involved with what he was writing than Flaubert. When he described Emma Bovary poisoning herself, he was so moved that he could taste arsenic on his own tongue and felt so poisoned himself that he vomited his dinner. And yet when he finally finished that scene, he had engineered it onto the page with an almost fanatical control. Once again, the writer's talent had produced an immortal passage out of passionate deliberation.

Flaubert would begin a single paragraph by setting down its general idea, with perhaps a few images (a risk always, for a brilliant image-making faculty he had; he wrote that he was devoured by metaphors as by vermin and spent his time crushing them). Then he wrote a first draft, reading it aloud for sound and sense (always read any sort of text out loud, the surest way to catch the feeble phrase, the trite adjective, the outworn image, the dull rhythm, the phony speech). Then he would rewrite, again and again, as a fine craftsman polishes over and over the same increasingly brilliant piece of maple or mahogany. Every word that did not act with energy was thrown away, until the paragraph was lean, tough, expressive. *Madame Bovary's* final version was written on 1,788 pages, but these were only the latest of many times that number of pages actually written. At times fifteen or twenty pages would be reduced to four.

Thus, when Flaubert said that he spent a week over two pages, he meant over the two finally perfected pages out of many more.

Flaubert may be the only man in history who told his girl friend, "You should write more coldly." This was a part of his advice that "we must be on our guard against that kind of intellectual overheating called inspiration, which often consists more largely of nervous emotion than of muscular strength . . . my brow is burning, sentences keep rushing into my head. . . . Instead of one idea I have six, and where the most simple type of exposition is called for I find myself writing similes and metaphors. I could keep going until tomorrow noon without fatigue." And yet he could follow such an outburst with the blunt advice, brief, wise, but taking most writers a lifetime to learn: "Everything should be done coldly, with poise." When putting down the word "hysterics" one day he was so carried away that he bellowed loudly and felt so sharply what Emma Bovary was going through that he was afraid of having hysterics himself.

Can it be that the French, more than any other people, are able to balance heat and cold, desire and deliberation, and make a single intense but controlled utterance? The modern poet, Paul Valéry, wrote that poetry must be a holiday of the mind and then said, with greater calm, that when he writes, "I proceed like a surgeon who sterilizes his hands and prepares the area to be operated on . . . clearing up the verbal situation."

The English seem more practical, if a little less dedicated to perfection. Novelist Joyce Cary described his process thus:

A finished book of mine starts usually perhaps ten years before as a character sketch and a bit of description; it goes on to an incident or so, it gathers subsidiary characters, and then perhaps I grow interested in it, and set out to give it form as a book. I sketch a plan; I may write the end, the middle, and the beginning and very often just in this order. That is, I decide how and where the book shall end, which is just as important to a book as to a play, and then I ask myself where are the most difficult turns in the book. Then I may write one of these difficult passages to see if it is viable. . . . I may stop there. But if it does work, then I may devise a beginning and finish the book.

How contrary to the old notion of inspiration to find Cary devising a beginning of a novel of which he has written bits in various parts and without order. This is evidence that what the writer is really doing is not so much writing a poem or play or story that he has firmly in mind, but rather is using his writing to discover what it truly is he is trying to say. Often he will not know until the final revision of the last page what he had been trying to do from the start.

One would hardly guess the zest and liveliness of Chekhov's mind if he had only seen a moody performance of *The Sea Gull*. Commenting on the new "decadent" writers he noted, "They're a lot of strong, healthy young men: what they need is to be sentenced to a few months hard labor! This new-art business is just a pack of nonsense. . . . There's nothing new in art except talent." Chekhov constantly wrote subjects for stories in moments taken from his medical practice ("Medicine is my lawful wife, literature my mistress. When I am tired of the one, I spend a night with the other"). One notebook contained 100 entries. Some of these are diverting: A building contractor of great frugality loathed paying repair bills. When he married, he chose an exceptionally healthy woman so that he would have no repair bills with her.

A writer should be as objective as a chemist, he commented, and have nothing to do with the subjective approach that most of us make in our everyday lives. And when he wrote that the writer should never sit down to his work until he felt cold as ice, he was remarkably like Flaubert. Any reader of Chekhov's short stories will be amazed to find how very simple were the original notes for two of the finest. "A cabdriver who has just lost his son has to go on working just the same. He tries to speak of his grief to his fares, but finds only indifference." Another equally famous story began with three little sentences. "Some officers on maneuvers are invited to a house where there are several young women. One of them kisses one of the officers, a shy and reserved young man, in the dark. He looks for her, but in vain." These are the plain, experienced reality, but the stories written out of them are the heightened overreality.

Poor Chekhov, tending the sick with his own fatal illness corrupting his lungs. When he died in Germany, his coffin was taken to Moscow in a baggage car marked "Oysters." Yet he never allowed a scrap of self-pity to interfere with the absolute integrity of his dedication to writing:

> My own experience is that once a story has been written, one has to cross out the beginning and the end. It is there that we authors do most of our lying. . . . One must always tear up the first half. I mean that seriously. Young writers begin by, as one says, "placing the story"—whereas the reader ought, on the contrary, to be able to grasp what it is all about by the way it is told, without any explanations from the author, from the conversation and the actions of the characters. . . . One must ruthlessly suppress everything that is not concerned with the subject. If, in the first chapter, you say there is a gun hanging on the wall, you should make quite sure that it is going to be used further on in the story.

Chekhov felt strongly the distinction between direct reality as it is lived and the imagined reality of art. In 1898 he went to a rehearsal of *The Sea Gull* at the Moscow Art Theater and was told by an actor that backstage there would be sounds of frogs croaking, grasshoppers scraping, and dogs barking. He asked why, and was told this would be realistic. But the theatre is not realism, it is art, he argued. If you put a real nose into a painting of a face, the nose will be realistic but the picture will be ruined. You do not use fiction to resolve the existence of God; you exhibit characters conducting lives and show the way in which they discuss God.

Similarly Tolstoy remarked that *Anna Karenina,* that massive novel, was just a simple story about a married woman who falls in love with an officer. This sort of reducing of any piece of writing to its essence is a part of that control over material which is indispensable to the practicing writer. Such definition comes out of enormous and confusing reaches of experience. No one has more imaginatively stated the mysterious and at the same time gritty nature of human existence than Virginia Woolf when she wrote that "life is a luminous halo, a semitransparent envelope surrounding us from the beginning."

Virginia Woolf also wrote a paragraph defining the nature of this envelope more precisely:

> Examine for a moment an ordinary mind on an ordinary day. The mind receives myriad impressions —trivial, fantastic, evanescent, or engraved with the sharpness of steel. From all sides they come, an incessant shower of innumerable atoms; and as they fall, as they shape themselves into the life of Monday or Tuesday, the accent falls differently from of old; the moment of importance came not here but there; so that, if the writer were a freeman and not a slave, if he could write what he chose, not what he must, if he could base his work upon his own feeling and not upon convention, there would be no plot, no comedy, no tragedy, no love interest, or catastrophe in the accepted style.

The simple, often gruntlike puffs of air which we call words must be used by the writer with such skill that they can bring to a reader, who cannot even hear whatever tone of voice the writer would give them, a form and sense that will move him. This is by no means so easy as lifting bricks all day or breaking stone. Flaubert testifies to that: "My head reels and my throat aches with chasing after, slogging over, delving into, turning 'round, groping after, and bellowing, in a hundred thousand different ways, a sentence that I've at last finished. It's good . . ." One sentence!

No one knew better the tortures or the necessity of this sort of harsh self-discipline than that most exuberant and debauched poet, Baudelaire. In his *Flowers of Evil*, he wrote, there was a cold and sinister beauty. How did that beauty happen? This first of the beatniks differed from his later brothers not in his contempt for the vulgarity of middle-class life, nor in his concern for the flaunting immorality that repudiated such life, but in his attitude toward his art. Yearning to have his book appear so that it could prove to his mother, his formidable father-in-law General Aupick, and his friends that he was an authentic poet, he nevertheless kept the printer waiting several months while he revised a few lines into perfection. It may actually be that much writing is created into excellence and then revised into greatness. This is true of the play, the story, the novel, the poem, the article, of whatever form men choose to make words move other men.

Robert Frost:
The Way to the Poem

by John Ciardi

A teacher-poet-critic examines a famous American poem and demonstrates that a discovery of how a poem means is more important to the reader than what it means.

Stopping by Woods on a Snowy Evening

BY ROBERT FROST

Whose woods these are I think I know.
His house is in the village though;
He will not see me stopping here
To watch his woods fill up with snow.

My little horse must think it queer
To stop without a farmhouse near
Between the wood and frozen lake
The darkest evening of the year.

He gives his harness bells a shake
To ask if there is some mistake.
The only other sound's the sweep
Of easy wind and downy flake.

The woods are lovely, dark and deep.
But I have promises to keep,
And miles to go before I sleep,
And miles to go before I sleep.

The School System has much to say these days of the virtue of reading widely, and not enough about the virtues of reading less but in depth. There are any number of reading lists for poetry, but there is not enough talk about individual poems. Poetry, finally, is one poem at a time. To read any one poem carefully is the ideal preparation for reading another. Only a poem can illustrate how poetry works.

Above, therefore, is a poem—one of the master lyrics of the English language, and almost certainly the best-known poem by an American poet. What happens in it?—which is to say, not *what* does it mean, but *how* does it mean? How does it go about being a human reenactment of a human experience? The author—perhaps the thousandth reader would need to be told—is Robert Frost.

Even the TV audience can see that this poem begins as a seemingly simple narration of a seemingly simple incident but ends by suggesting meanings far beyond anything specifically referred to in the narrative. And even readers with only the most casual interest in poetry might be made to note the additional fact that, though the poem suggests those larger meanings, it is very careful never to abandon its pretense to being simple narration. There is duplicity at work. The poet pretends to be talking about one thing, and all the while he is talking about many others.

Many readers are forever unable to accept the poet's essential duplicity. It is almost safe to say that a poem is never about what it seems to be about. As much could be said of the proverb. The bird in the hand, the rolling stone, the stitch in time never (except by an artful double-deception) intend any sort of statement about birds, stones, or sewing. The incident of this poem, one must conclude, is at root a metaphor.

Duplicity aside, this poem's movement from the specific to the general illustrates one of the basic formulas of all poetry. Such a grand poem as Arnold's "Dover Beach" and such lesser, though unfortunately better-known, poems as Longfellow's "The Village Blacksmith" and Holmes's "The Chambered Nautilus" are built on the same progression. In these three poems, however, the generalization is markedly set apart from the specific narration, and even seems additional to the telling rather than intrinsic to it. It is this sense of division one has in mind in speaking of "a tacked-on moral."

There is nothing wrong-in-itself with a tacked-on moral. Frost, in fact, makes excellent use of the device at times.

In this poem, however, Frost is careful to let the whatever-the-moral-is grow out of the poem itself. When the action ends the poem ends. There is no epilogue and no explanation. Everything pretends to be about the narrated incident. And that pretense sets the basic tone of the poem's performance of itself.

The dramatic force of that performance is best observable, I believe, as a progression in three scenes.

In scene one, which coincides with stanza one, a man—a New Englander—is driving his sleigh somewhere at night. It is snowing, and as the man passes a dark patch of woods he stops to watch the snow descend into the darkness. We know, moreover, that the man is familiar with those parts (he knows who owns the woods and where the owner lives), and we know that no one has seen him stop. As scene one forms itself in the theatre of the mind's eye, therefore, it serves to establish some as yet unspecified relation between the man and the woods.

It is necessary, however, to stop here for a long parenthesis: Even so simple an opening statement raises any number of questions. It is impossible to address all the questions that rise from the poem stanza by stanza, but two that arise from stanza one illustrate the sort of thing one might well ask of the poem detail by detail.

Why, for example, does the man not say what errand he is on? What is the force of leaving the errand generalized? He might just as well have told us that he was going to the general store, or returning from it with a jug of molasses he had promised to bring Aunt Harriet and two suits of long underwear he had promised to bring the hired man. Frost, moreover, can handle homely detail to great effect. He preferred to leave his motive generalized. Why?

And why, on the other hand, does he say so much about knowing the absent owner of the woods and where he lives? Is it simply that one set of details happened-in whereas another did not? To speak of things "happening-in" is to assault the integrity of a poem. Poetry cannot be discussed meaningfully unless one can assume that everything in the poem—every last comma and variant spelling—is in it by the poet's specific act of choice. Only bad poets allow into their poems what is haphazard or cheaply chosen.

The errand, I will venture a bit brashly for lack of space,

is left generalized in order the more aptly to suggest *any* errand in life and, therefore, life itself. The owner is there because he is one of the forces of the poem. Let it do to say that the force he represents is the village of mankind (that village at the edge of winter) from which the poet finds himself separated (has separated himself?) in his moment by the woods (and to which, he recalls finally, he has promised to keep). The owner is he-who-lives-in-his-village-house, thereby locked away from the poet's awareness of the-time-the-snow-tells as it engulfs and obliterates the world the village man allows himself to believe he "owns." Thus, the owner is a representative of an order of reality from which the poet has divided himself for the moment, though to a certain extent he ends by re-uniting with it. Scene one, therefore, establishes not only a relation between the man and the woods, but the fact that the man's relation begins with his separation (though momentarily) from mankind.

End parenthesis one, begin parenthesis two.

Still considering the first scene as a kind of dramatic performance of forces, one must note that the poet has meticulously matched the simplicity of his language to the pretended simplicity of the narrative. Clearly, the man stopped because the beauty of the scene moved him, but he neither tells us that the scene is beautiful nor that he is moved. A bad writer, always ready to overdo, might have written: "The vastness gripped me, filling my spirit with the slow steady sinking of the snow's crystalline perfection into the glimmerless profundities of the hushed primeval wood." Frost's avoidance of such a spate illustrates two principles of good writing. The first, he has stated himself in "The Mowing": "Anything *more* than the truth would have seemed too weak" (italics mine). Understatement is one of the basic sources of power in English poetry. The second principle is to let the action speak for itself. A good novelist does not tell us that a given character is good or bad (at least not since the passing of the Dickens tradition): he shows us the character in action and then, watching him, we know. Poetry, too, has fictional obligations: even when the characters are ideas and metaphors rather than people, they must be *characterized in action*. A poem does not *talk about* ideas; it *enacts* them. The force of the poem's performance, in fact, is precisely to act out (and thereby to make us act out emphatically—that is, to *feel out,* that is, to *identify with*) the speaker and why he stopped. The man is the principal actor in this little "drama of why" and in scene one he is the only character, though as noted, he is somehow related to the absent owner.

End second parenthesis.

In scene two (stanzas two and three) a *foil* is introduced. In fiction and drama, a foil is a character who "plays against" a more important character. By presenting a different point of view or an opposed set of motives, the foil moves the more important character to react in ways that might not have found expression without such opposition. The more important character is thus more fully revealed—to the reader and to himself. The foil is the horse.

The horse forces the question, Why did the man stop? Until it occurs to him that his "little horse must think it queer" he had not asked himself for reasons. He had simply stopped. But the man finds himself faced with the question he imagines the horse to be asking: What *is* there to stop for out there in the cold, away from bin and stall (house and village and mankind?) and all that any self-respecting beast could value on such a night? In sensing that other view, the man is forced to examine his own more deeply.

In stanza two the question arises only as a feeling within the man. In stanza three, however (still scene two), the horse acts. He gives his harness bells a shake. "What's wrong?" he seems to say. "What are we waiting for?"

By now, obviously, the horse—without losing its identity as horse—has also become a symbol. (A symbol is something that stands for something else.) Whatever that something else may be, it certainly begins at that order of life that does not understand why a man stops in the wintry middle of nowhere to watch the snow come down. (Can one fail to sense by now that the dark and the snow-fall symbolize a death-wish, however momentary, i.e., that hunger for final rest and oblivion that a man may feel, but not a beast?)

So by the end of scene two the performance has given dramatic force to three elements that work upon the man. There is his relation to the world of the owner. There is his relation to the brute world of the horse. And there is that third presence of the unownable world, the movement of the all-engulfing snow across all the orders of life, the man's, the owner's, and the horse's—with the difference that the man knows of that second dark-within-the-dark of which the horse cannot, and the owner will not, know.

The man ends scene two with all these forces working upon him simultaneously. He feels himself moved to a decision. And he feels a last call from the darkness: "the sweep/ Of easy wind and downy flake." It would be so easy and so downy to go into the woods and let himself be covered over.

But scene three (stanza four) produces a fourth force. This fourth force can be given many names. It is certainly better, in fact, to give it many names than to attempt to limit it to one. It is social obligation, or personal commitment, or duty, or just the realization that a man cannot indulge a mood forever. All of these and more. But finally he has a simple decision to make. He may go into the woods and let the darkness and the snow swallow him from the world of beast and man. Or he must move on. And unless he is going to stop here forever, it is time to remember that he has a long way to go and that he had best be getting there. (So there is something to be said for the horse, too.)

There and only then, his question driven more and more deeply into himself by these cross-forces, does the man venture a comment on what attracted him: "The woods are lovely, dark and deep." His mood lingers over the thought of that lovely dark-and-deep (as do the very syllables in which he phrases the thought), but the final decision is to put off the mood and move on. He has his man's way to go and his man's obligations to tend to before he can yield. He has miles to go before his sleep. He repeats that thought and the performance ends.

But why the repetition? The first time Frost says, "And miles to go before I sleep," there can be little doubt that the primary meaning is: "I have a long way to go before I get to bed tonight." The second time he says it, however, "miles to go" and "sleep" are suddenly transformed into symbols. What are those "something-elses" the symbols

stand for? Hundreds of people have tried to ask Mr. Frost
that question and he has always turned it away. He has
turned it away *because he cannot answer it.* He could
answer some part of it. But some part is not enough.

For a symbol is like a rock dropped into a pool: it sends
out ripples in all directions, and the ripples are in motion.
Who can say where the last ripple disappears? One may
have a sense that he knows the approximate center point
of the ripples, the point at which the stone struck the
water. Yet even then he has trouble marking it surely.
How does one make a mark on water? Oh very well—the
center point of that second "miles to go" is probably approximately in the neighborhood of being close to meaning,
perhaps, "the road of life"; and the second "before I sleep"
is maybe that close to meaning "before I take my final
rest," the rest in darkness that seemed so temptingly dark-
and-deep for the moment of the mood. But the ripples
continue to move and the light to change on the water,
and the longer one watches the more changes he sees.
Such shifting-and-being-at-the-same-instant is of the very
sparkle and life of poetry. One experiences it as one
experiences life, for everytime he looks at an experience he
sees something new, and he sees it change as he watches
it. And that sense of continuity in fluidity is one of the
primary kinds of knowledge, and one that only the arts can
teach, poetry foremost among them.

Frost himself certainly did not ask what that repeated
last line meant. It came to him and he received it. He "felt
right" about it. And what he "felt right" about was in no
sense a "meaning" that, say, an essay could apprehend, but
an act of experience that could be fully presented only by
the dramatic enactment of forces which is the performance
of the poem.

Now look at the poem in another way. Did Frost know
what he was going to do when he began? Considering the
poem simply as an act of skill, as a piece of juggling, one
cannot fail to respond to the magnificent turn at the end
where, with one flip, seven of the simplest words in the
language suddenly dazzle full of never-ending waves of
thought and feeling. Or, more precisely, of felt-thought. Certainly an equivalent stunt by a juggler—could there be an

equivalent—would bring the house down. Was it to cap his performance with that grand stunt that Frost wrote the poem?

Far from it. The obvious fact is that *Frost could not have known he was going to write those lines until he wrote them.* Then a second fact must be registered: *he wrote them because, for the fun of it, he had got himself into trouble.*

Frost, like every good poet, began by playing a game with himself. The most usual way of writing a four-line stanza with four feet to the line is to rhyme the third line with the first, and the fourth with the second. Even that much rhyme is so difficult in English that many poets and almost all of the anonymous ballad makers do not bother to rhyme the first and third lines at all, settling for two rhymes in four lines as good enough. For English is a rhyme-poor language. In Italian and in French, for example, so many words end with the same sounds that rhyming is relatively easy—so easy that many modern French and Italian poets do not bother to rhyme at all. English, being a more agglomerate language, has far more final sounds, hence fewer of them rhyme. When an Italian poet writes a line ending with "vita" (life) he has literally hundreds of rhyme choices available. When an English poet writes "life" at the end of a line he can summon "strife, wife, knife, fife, rife," and then he is in trouble. No "life-strife" and "life-rife" and "life-wife" seem to offer a combination of possible ideas that can be related by more than just the rhyme. Inevitably, therefore, the poets have had to work and rework these combinations until the sparkle has gone out of them. The reader is normally tired of such rhyme-led associations. When he encounters "life-strife" he is certainly entitled to suspect that the poet did not really want to say "strife"—that had there been in English such a word as, say, "hife," meaning "infinite peace and harmony," the poet would as gladly have used that word instead of "strife." Thus, the reader feels that the writing is haphazard, that the rhyme is making the poet say things he does not really feel, and which, therefore, the reader does not feel except as boredom. One likes to see the rhymes fall into place, but he must end with the belief that it is the poet who is deciding what is said and not the rhyme scheme that is forcing the saying.

So rhyme is a kind of game, and an especially difficult one in English. As in every game, the fun of the rhyme is to set one's difficulties high and then to meet them skilfully. As Frost himself once defined freedom, it consists of "moving easy in harness."

In "Stopping by Woods on a Snowy Evening" Frost took a long chance. He decided to rhyme not two lines in each stanza, but three. Not even Frost could have sustained that much rhyme in a long poem (as Dante, for example, with the advantage of writing in Italian, sustained triple rhyme for thousands of lines in *The Divine Comedy*). Frost would have known instantly, therefore, when he took the original chance, that he was going to write a short poem. He would have had that much foretaste of it.

So the first stanza emerged rhymed *a-a-b-a*. And with the sure sense that this was to be a short poem, Frost decided to take an additional chance and to redouble: in English three rhymes in four lines is more than enough; there is no need to rhyme the fourth line. For the fun of it, however, Frost set himself to pick up that loose rhyme and to weave it into the pattern, thereby accepting the all but impossible burden of quadruple rhyme.

The miracle is that it worked. Despite the enormous freight of rhyme, the poem not only came out as a neat pattern, but managed to do so with no sense of strain. Every word and every rhyme falls into place as naturally and as inevitably as if there were no rhyme restricting the poet's choices.

That ease-in-difficulty is certainly inseparable from the success of the poem's performance. One watches the skillman juggle three balls, then four, then five, and every addition makes the trick more wonderful. But unless he makes the hard trick seem as easy as an easy trick, then all is lost.

The real point, however, is not only that Frost took on a hard rhyme-trick and made it seem easy. It is rather as if the juggler, carried away, had tossed up one more ball than he could really handle, and then amazed himself by actually handling it. So with the real triumph of this poem. Frost could not have known what a stunning effect his repetition of the last line was going to produce. He could not even know he was going to repeat the line. He simply found himself up against a difficulty he almost certainly had not foreseen and he had to improvise to meet it. For in picking up the rhyme from the third line of stanza one and carrying it over into stanza two, he had created an endless chain-link form within which each stanza left a hook sticking out for the next stanza to hang on. So by stanza four, feeling the poem rounding to its end, Frost had to do something about that extra rhyme.

He might have tucked it back into a third line rhyming with the *know-though-snow* of stanza one. He could thus have rounded the poem out to the mathematical symmetry of using each rhyme four times. But though such a device might be defensible in theory, a rhyme repeated after eleven lines is so far from its original rhyme sound that its feeling as rhyme must certainly be lost. And what good is theory if the reader is not moved by the writing?

It must have been in some such quandary that the final repetition suggested itself—a suggestion born of the very difficulties the poet had let himself in for. So there is that point beyond mere ease in handling a hard thing, the point at which the very difficulty offers the poet the opportunity to do better than he knew he could. What, aside from having that happen to oneself, could be more self-delighting than to participate in its happening by one's reader-identification with the poem?

And by now a further point will have suggested itself: that the human-insight of the poem and the technicalities of its poetic artifice are inseparable. Each feeds the other. That interplay is the poem's meaning, a matter not of WHAT DOES IT MEAN, for no one can ever say entirely what a good poem means, but of HOW DOES IT MEAN, a process one can come much closer to discussing.

There is a necessary epilogue. Mr. Frost has often discussed this poem on the platform, or more usually in the course of a long-evening-after a talk. Time and again I have heard him say that he just wrote it off, that it just came to him, and that he set it down as it came.

Once at Bread Loaf, however, I heard him add one very essential piece to the discussion of how it "just came." One night, he said, he had sat down after supper to work at a long piece of blank verse. The piece never worked out, but Mr. Frost found himself so absorbed in it that, when next he looked up, dawn was at his window. He rose, crossed to the window, stood looking out for a few minutes, and *then* it was that "Stopping by Woods" suddenly "just came," so that all he had to do was cross the room and write it down.

Robert Frost is the sort of artist who hides his traces. I know of no Frost worksheets anywhere. If someone has raided his wastebasket in secret, it is possible that such worksheets exist somewhere, but Frost would not willingly allow anything but the finished product to leave him. Almost certainly, therefore, no one will ever know what was in that piece of unsuccessful blank verse he had been working at with such concentration, but I for one would stake my life that could that worksheet be uncovered, it would be found to contain the germinal stuff of "Stopping by Woods"; that what was a-simmer in him all night without finding its proper form, suddenly, when he let his still-occupied mind look away, came at him from a different direction, offered itself in a different form, and that finding that form exactly right the impulse proceeded to marry itself to the new shape in one of the most miraculous performances of English lyricism.

And that, too—whether or not one can accept so hypothetical a discussion—is part of HOW the poem means. It means that marriage to the perfect form, the poem's shapen declaration of itself, its moment's monument fixed beyond all possibility of change. And thus, finally, in every truly good poem, "How does it mean?" must always be answered "Triumphantly." Whatever the poem "is about," *how* it means is always how Genesis means: the word become a form, and the form become a thing, and—when the becoming is true—the thing become a part of the knowledge and experience of the race forever.

So Long As the Theater Can Do Miracles

by Tyrone Guthrie

An actor-director supports, by recalling some of his own great and near great evenings as a spectator, the theory that "prefabricated mass-distributed" drama lacks the excitement, the tensions and even the mishaps of a live performance before a perceptive audience.

People always seem to be worrying about the theater. It is sick; it is dying. I suppose all this concern reflects affection or, at any rate, a feeling that if the Fabulous Invalid were finally to pass away, there would be a sense of bereavement.

For my part, I am not quite convinced that drama is as indispensable to human existence as meat and drink; life can be supported without it, but only just. It is almost the first form of human expression—for what is babyhood's universal game of peekaboo but a pretending, for dramatic purposes, to be invisible, the making of an effective "exit" and a no less effective "reentrance"? Drama underlies every social and communal experience: Mr. Jones "dramatizes" the occurrences of his working day when he gets home at night and, in return, Mrs. J. "dramatizes" her exploits at sink and supermarket and Junior's marvelous repartee to teacher. What are the little ceremonials attendant upon weddings, funerals, parties, even ordinary meals and casual drinks, but an attempt to make these occasions more significant by dramatizing them?

Naturally, the form in which drama is presented will vary from time to time and from place to place, as it always has. The Greek theater differed in form from the medieval, the medieval from the Elizabethan; Molière's theater again was different, and our own is different again and still changing, still fluid. What an audience receives keeps changing; and so does what an audience gives.

Right now, we are in an era when the form of drama is dominated by the ideas of massive distribution. It is considered important and desirable that a dramatic performance should be simultaneously available to many millions of people, in widely scattered places. This is probably because we have only recently—during the last fifty years or so—discovered technical means to make a performance so available. Therefore the idea still has the charm of novelty. But already the novelty is beginning to lose its gloss. Enormously wide availability begins to be commonplace; and now we begin to see that it has many grave disadvantages.

For instance, a drama which must simultaneously appeal to people in Delhi, Durban, Dublin and Dallas, to people of the most widely differing cultures and degrees of education—such a drama, if it is to please so many kinds of people somewhat, can please no single group very intensely. This then becomes a cue for the Jeremiahs: "Movies and television have killed the 'live' drama; and mechanized drama has many grave disadvantages. The Fabulous Invalid is sicker than ever."

Anxiety is catching. Every now and again, even the stanchest believer in the Invalid's survival needs reassurance. I have just had such reassurance: a most life-giving, thrilling performance at the Old Vic in London of Ibsen's *Peer Gynt*.

Now I am not for a moment suggesting that art is the only source of thrilling, life-giving experience; nor even that, among the arts, the theater is the sole, or even the supreme, source of such experience. But there are, I think, certain respects in which drama can be supremely stimulating, and certain respects in which, of all forms of drama, "live" performance still excels all others.

Painting, sculpture and literature have certain important advantages over the performing arts. The painter, sculptor and writer express themselves in their own time, in conditions which, to a considerable extent, they can determine for themselves. And their work, once created, is not importantly governed by public response. A picture or a book does not change because a group of people dislikes or misunderstands it. Its reputation and its commercial value may be ruined but, so long as the canvas remains intact or the book remains accessible, even if difficult of access, the idea expressed by the artist remains unaffected. And there is always a possibility that, with changing taste, what was formerly despised may come to be appreciated.

Performance, on the other hand, takes place at a time and in an environment which the performer can rarely choose; and the performance lives or dies by the reaction of the audience. The very nature of a performer makes him abnormally sensitive to the reaction of his audience. His self-expression is inextricably bound up with the desire to please, to be accepted. Those who create works of art destined for performance—composers and dramatists—must be aware of this. They must know that their work will not fully be brought to life until it is performed, and not unless the performance is acceptable to an audience. To this extent, they are less free of the tyranny of public opinion than painters or literary men. But, in their turn, composers and dramatists are more free from such tyranny than are actors, singers, dancers, instrumentalists.

The first public performance of *La Traviata* was a failure. The work has subsequently been performed tens of thousands of times all over the world and with triumphant success. But, for the lady who originally sang the leading role, there was no subsequent triumph. She had her chance and missed it—irretrievably.

Movie and television drama are in this respect more merciful to the performer. To begin with, the worst blunders can generally be eliminated by cutting and retakes before the product is seen by the public. Second, insofar as the film or the tape remains in existence, there is always a chance that a performance which was unappreciated at first may subsequently meet with sympathy and comprehension.

This is convenient and comforting, but must occasionally be embarrassing. It cannot be pleasant to catch yourself in an ephemeral drama whose situations seemed poignant thirty years ago, but now are utterly boring, and there you are carrying on to beat the band in the preposterous hairdo and clothes which were the *dernier cri de 1933*. And yet—who knows? Another thirty years may pass and the whole thing will be starting to take on the charming air of an antique. And after three times thirty more, your descendants may be acclaiming the whole silly thing as a classic and your performance will be "immortal."

It is possible. But unlikely. The reasons behind the making of most mass-distributed drama preclude immortality. They are strictly short-term. Also, the mere fact that the performance is prefabricated reduces its value. Its quality is already determined; it holds no surprise. There is no element of risk. We know that the skater in a film will not break a leg; the actors will not "dry up"; their wigs will not come unstuck; the scenery will not fall down.

But in the theater this element of trick and suspense is important and is part of the charm. Wigs come all too easily unstuck; for a performance to go through from beginning to end without mistake or mishap of any kind is quite a feat. But just to say that no mishap has occurred is to put the matter in a very negative way; the positive fact is that almost every performance has its element of virtuosity—something extremely difficult has been brilliantly achieved.

In vaudeville, we applaud the man who balances a seventy-two-piece dinner service of valuable china, on a tray, on a billiard cue, on the tip of his nose. It may not be the highest flight of art but it does represent a high degree of virtuosity—the double octaves in Liszt's "Campanella," the brilliance of a Bach toccata. In opera, it is the roulades of a Sutherland or a Callas which "bring down the house." They, too, do not represent the highest flights in art, but we all know that they are way beyond our own capacity in the bath; rightly we applaud what we can appreciate—exceptional gifts developed with exceptional application.

In the theater, likewise, virtuoso performance is the single most exciting and most popular feature. And the most exciting feature of virtuoso performance is the possibility of failure. One day—and oh, may we be there to see it!—the seventy-two-piece dinner service *will* smash; Rubinstein *will* make a hash of "La Campanella"; Callas, Sutherland, Olivier *will* fail to deliver.

In prefabricated, mass-distributed performances, this thrill is missing. It is an important reason why they so signally lack the Sense of Occasion.

Now let us return to *Peer Gynt*. It was exciting partly because it was a good performance of a masterpiece, rarely

put on because of its massive scale and extreme difficulty.
Yet this meant that there were many pitfalls. Not all were
avoided. Here and there, it must be admitted, there were
longueurs, even here and there absurdities, but never long
enough or gross enough to spoil the evening.

It was like being in a ship in a storm. We pitched, we
rolled, now and again we wallowed in the trough of a
wave, now and again we shipped a good deal of water.
But we always had confidence in our vessel and her crew.
We knew that soon we should again be triumphant on the
wave's crest. And we appreciated that a dangerous voyage
is far more thrilling than a calm and tame one. Indeed, the
spice of the evening was that again and again the vessel
righted herself after seeming about to founder with all
hands.

Another reason for the evening's thrill was that it was
such hard work. It lasted nearly four hours; by the end
of three, my head was aching with the strain of "keeping
up"; and I know the play extremely well. The heads of
those who were seeing it for the first time must have been
simply bursting. But they were "keeping up"; you could
tell that by the way they laughed almost as the actors
cracked a joke, or by the tension of the emotional passages
when the silence was such that a pin dropping would have
crashed like a falling crowbar.

We all enjoyed ourselves so much just because we had
spent ourselves so prodigally. We value what costs a lot,
not what is cheap. We came out after a good laugh, a good
cry, a good stretch of the imagination, feeling tired but
happy, a feeling exactly analogous to that which follows
strenuous but enjoyable physical exertion.

The happiness comes partly just from the fact of relax-
ation after effort, but partly because the reward of the effort is a harvest of recollected sights and sounds and ideas
more high-colored and at once more orderly and various
than those of "real" life. Most of all, the happiness comes
because pent-up energies have been released. It is this release, I think, to which Aristotle refers when he writes of
the "purgative" nature of tragedy.

This release seldom follows a commercial entertainment,
because it seldom makes sufficient demand upon our energies. Those who purvey commercial entertainment know

very well that we are all lazy most of the time, and many of us are lazy all the time. Strenuous entertainment does not pay so well as the kind which makes minimal demands upon our faculties. The most paying of all is the kind that can be received with no effort at all, that permits us to take in the entertainment through the pores of the skin at a level comfortably below consciousness. This is why most Television Entertainment is as it is.

Peer Gynt also offered in no small degree the excitement of virtuoso performance. The name-part is enormous. At the beginning of the evening, Peer is a youth of eighteen, at the end an old man of seventy. The part makes immense demands not only on the imagination but on the physical energy of the actor. At the Old Vic, the part was played by Leo McKern, an Australian in his early forties. He is no matinee idol. He is a dumpy, bun-faced person whose profile will set no girlish heart aflame. But what energy! What a voice! He can coo like a dove, roar like a lion, shriek like a banshee, rattle like a machine gun, sing like an angel and curse like—well, as only Australians can.

I suppose anyone who goes to the theater fairly often has his store of Great Moments. But in this context I am concerned less with great moments than with a more sustained exhilaration. The Great Moments are nearly always connected with the personality of an actor or actress, and there is nothing wrong with that. The impact of a great personality is probably the most exciting and memorable single element in any theatrical experience. But such an impact is usually rememberable only in fragmentary form; how she looked in the death scene; his cry of recognition; the moment when they realized . . .

But I am thinking less of great moments and more of whole evenings of exhilaration. Naturally, these become fewer and farther between as, with advancing years, we become less impressionable. I find that most of my own great evenings in the theater occurred a good many years ago.

I recall *Jedermann (Everyman)*, at Salzburg, unforgettably staged by Reinhardt on the steps of the cathedral against its baroque west front. In the brilliant sunshine there was little attempt at illusion. I don't think that many people can have been deceived into thinking that the actor

in a skull-like mask really was Death, or that any of the
events of the play were really taking place. That did not
make the performance any the less impressive and com-
pelling. We were witnessing a reenactment of ordered
events which we were not supposed to mistake for a
spontaneous enactment.

So, I think, it must be with any great theatrical expression. No person of the least sophistication mistakes figment
for reality. The figment must, it is true, suggest an identi-
fiable reality: we must be able to recognize that the actor
playing Hamlet represents a prince, in reaction to the
ghost of his murdered father, to the usurpation of the
throne by his uncle, to the murder of his father and adul-
tery with his mother by that same uncle. Hamlet's reaction
to these things and others, though it is often mysterious,
even inexplicable, must be sufficiently plausible to convince us of his humanity and to engage not merely our
interest but our sympathy.

My own greatest evening with *Hamlet* was when Gielgud
played the part many years ago in a revival directed by
himself. I have been fortunate enough to see many dozens
of impersonations of Hamlet; some of them were brilliant
and none—not even high-school boys, not even a high-
school girl—was entirely without interest. Olivier was
the most vigorous, Barrymore the most romantic, Evans
the most consistently audible, Plummer the wittiest.

Gielgud was the most musical and the most royal; his
was for me the most satisfactory embodiment of the part
and his production the best realization of the play. The evening spent in the company of this Hamlet was one of the
splendid evenings of my life.

Other great evenings for me have been *Noah* by André
Obey, performed under the direction of Michel Saint-Denis
by La Compagnie de Quinze; and a performance in Glasgow by a Jewish amateur group of *The Long Christmas
Dinner* by Thornton Wilder.

Oddly enough, though I have seen most of the important
productions of the last ten or twelve years, I have experienced no great occasions in the theater in New York.
There have been moments, breathtaking moments, especially
visually. There have been Ethel Merman and Ruth Gor-
don and Bert Lahr. There has been a great deal of splen-

didly organized high spirits and fun. *My Fair Lady* was a brilliant piece of work but not, in my opinion, a *great* evening; it was an enormously skillful popularization of a fifty-year-old comedy with a sprinkling of easily memorable, because highly derivative, tunes. It was a gay evening, a pleasant evening, but not a great one.

West Side Story was the most technically accomplished performance I ever hope to see. But I do not regard it as a great evening because it was evident that its gifted creators were stooping to conquer the popular audience rather than expressing what they had it in them to say about the theme. All in all, I have seen little on Broadway which had even the ambition to attempt a great evening. *Long Day's Journey into Night* was a good try and, of all I have seen, the only qualifier for top-league status.

I had almost forgotten: Laurette Taylor in *The Glass Menagerie*. Her performance was probably the best of its kind which any of us will ever see. The play, I believe, was better than a rather dim production permitted it to seem. Maybe this was a Great Evening. I would feel more sure if I could recall more about it than the central character. She, however, remains about a thousand times more vivid than most of the so-called real people whom my path has crossed.

You may be present when a painter is at work; you may watch a writer as his pen moves across the page or, more likely, as he whacks the typewriter; you are only watching the mechanics of creation, a relatively unimportant part of the whole process. Performance is different. When you are there, when you "assist," as the French so rightly express it, as a violinist gives a great account of a masterpiece or as an actor transforms himself into Hamlet, Harpagon, Faust or Peer Gynt, it is as though you were there when God said, "Let there be light." Indeed God, through his minister, is saying, "Let there be light."

Now the supreme thrill of the theater is that this miracle does not always come to pass. Sometimes the failure is the performer's fault; he may be unable to muster the physical resource, the mental concentration required. But more often it is the fault of the audience. Performance is a two-way traffic. The greatest performer can only be great when the reaction of the audience permits greatness.

Inadequacy is not always an audience's fault. It is hard to be enthusiastic if your feet are cold or damp. It is hard to concentrate if there are distracting noises—a road drill outside, talkative ushers, rustling candy-papers. Moreover, in every audience there will be a certain number of "duds": some too dull to appreciate anything, some who are pre-occupied with business or family cares, love, toothache or other disease. If these people are not too numerous or spiritually powerful, they can be conquered by the rest and gradually fused into the single composite mass personality of an Audience. But sometimes it is the duds who conquer; an infectious lethargy spreads, inattention is expressed by coughs and fidgets.

It is one of the unfortunate features of public performance that the first night is all-important for the reputation of all concerned. Opening-night audiences are murder. An Important Occasion always attracts a lot of would-be fashionable sillies, who want to be "in the swim" and who are more concerned to draw attention to themselves than to con-tribute to the quality of the performance. There are the professional critics, rightly detached, wrongly, though un-derstandably, blasé. Then there is the curious jarring an-tiphony set up by the professional "knockers," the death-watch beetles, mostly disappointed professionals, rejected lovers of the muse, of whom there are always a few dozen at any important artistic occasion.

As a counterpoint to these, and equally disturbing, is the anxious partisanship of the performers' friends, so deter-mined to make things "go" that again and again you may distinguish the cackling of the author's mother, the braying of the leading lady's husband, and, at the end, the pro-ducer conducting the ushers, the understudies and a group of trusties in a well-rehearsed fusillade of acclaim.

All this makes for distraction and disharmony. Occasion-ally, the tension stimulates the performers; far more often they give a flurried, hectic, self-conscious account of them-selves. The performance can never be steady and normal, never the kind on which any just or reasoned judgment should be based.

And now, finally, it occurs to me that perhaps the great-est thing of all at *Peer Gynt* was in the self-congratula-tory department: we were a splendid audience. Consequently, we evoked from the company the splendid performance which we deserved. We were part of the creative process.

This, I believe, is why live performance will never die. Drama or music can, of course, be much more widely distributed by movies, radio, television, gramophone and so on, and such reproductions can have a technical gloss never quite attainable in the rough and tumble of live performance. And I do not underestimate the importance of this. But these mechanically reproduced performances can never create the all-important Sense of Occasion—none of them can offer to spectator or listener the possibility of *creative participation*.

At the *Peer Gynt* that night at the Old Vic, each one of us—whether on stage or in front, whether in great degree like Leo McKern, in lesser degree like the small-part players and the stage technicians, or in least degree, like myself and the rest of the audience—each of us said, "Let there be light," and there was light. The exhilaration was extraordinary, but not unique. It has happened a million times before and will happen a million times again. And so long as it can happen, the Fabulous Invalid will never die; indeed, I suggest that the reports of his sickness have been considerably exaggerated.

TV Shows Are Not
Supposed To Be Good

by David Karp

*A television writer argues that television shows are de-
signed to make money and that a great creative medium
is being wasted because viewers do not switch off their
sets when bad shows come on them.*

My mother enjoyed no reputation as a sage, except
within the circle of my family, but she summed up television when Lee DeForest was still muttering about the
obstinacy of the cathode ray tube that wouldn't work. She
said, "Rich people aren't smarter than poor people. They
are just smarter sooner." My trouble was (is) that I am
still not smarter sooner.

In 1941 I was working for the W.P.A. in the Police Ath-
letic League, and my office was on one of the upper floors
of the 23d Precinct station in East Harlem. It was there I
saw my first television set—and my first television programs.
I recall that the room set aside for TV was crowded with
earnest, hard-breathing air-raid wardens who sat and
watched closed-circuit TV programs which demonstrated
the best way of dealing with fire bombs. Cops who were
assigned to watch such instruction stood in sober silence.

But civil defense indoctrination was not the only thing
you could see on the set. I drifted in one afternoon and
found several policemen sitting there, entranced and chor-
tling. The air-raid wardens were gone, and on the screen
there flickered an ancient film. For all I know, it was
Robert Flaherty's *Moana of the South Seas*. I was there
long enough to determine that the heroine wore a topless
sarong and the cops were watching with a fascination and
interest that they had never shown over the handling of in-
cendiary bombs.

If God had intended me to be a wealthy man, He might

then have smitten me with the blinding vision similar to those He visited upon Henry Ford, "Cheap Cars!"; F. W. Woolworth, "Nothing Over Ten Cents!"; Harvey Firestone, "Cook Rubber!"; Billy Rose, "Buy A.T.&T.!" To me He would have said: "Movies for TV!"

Maybe He did say something like that. But He never said it to me. I know it was said to someone, because look at the current TV schedule. Maybe it was to Lew Wasserman of MCA and Universal Pictures.

Merle Miller and Evan Rhodes, in a kind of agonized exposé of television called *Only You, Dick Darling!*, lamented that television lacerated the sensibilities of writers. So it does. It also lacerates the sensibilities of directors, musicians, actors and producers, as well as those of viewers, critics, intellectuals, and all other kinds of people. It is, in fact, the cheekiest, vulgarest, noisiest, most disgraceful form of public entertainment since bear-baiting, dog-fighting and the seasonal Czarist Russian pogrom.

And yet 92.8 percent of American families (67.1 million) have at least one TV set, against 80 percent with telephones. Television grows more and more awful, yet a projection by the National Association of Broadcasters indicates that within the next five years there will be "penetration" into the hold-out 7.2 percent of homes which may bring the number of those without TV down to 1 or 2 percent.

In 1950, when I first came into television, advertisers were spending 170.8 million dollars in network, spot and local station commercials. In 1964, the total was 2.29 billion dollars. In 1950, there were 97 commercial stations in operation. This year there are 572, and with the opening up of the UHF (Ultra-High Frequency) spectrum, the number of stations may double. If they double, all the other figures may double—sets, viewers, dollars, and so on.

If you find large numbers as tiresome as I do, you may wonder vaguely what it all means. It means, to begin with, that you will never be rich. There are thousands of intelligent, well-educated, carefully combed and curried men who love such numbers and who write them down and add them up and who chuckle softly over them. They are numbers which have meaning and importance to these men.

These men couldn't care less about art forms or entertainment or esthetics. And yet those domiciled at industry headquarters in California faithfully attend U.C.L.A.'s serious dramatic productions, are visitors and contributors to the new Los Angeles Art Museum and deeply resent the charge that Los Angeles is a cultural desert. They pride themselves on the musical riches of Southern California, as typified by the presence of Jascha Heifetz and Gregor Piatigorsky. Even Henry Miller is a Californian. How much culture can you want? Their big point, of course, is that all this culture belongs in universities, in little theaters—or even in big theaters—and certainly not on TV (except on educational channels). TV is not an art form or a culture channel; it is an advertising medium.

Executives of MCA (once the giant agent of show business and then, by Justice Department fiat, a producer of films) have proudly boasted to *Forbes* magazine that the reason they make so much money is that they don't worry about making "art films." They leave the making of "art films" to studios like MGM and 20th-Century Fox. They themselves are strictly in television and film-making to make money. Obviously, if their object is to make money—and they do make money—it seems a bit churlish and un-American of people who watch television to complain that their shows are so lousy. They are not *supposed* to be any good. They are supposed to make money.

In all justice to MCA, their spokesmen were talking to interviewers from *Forbes,* which is published for "hard headed" businessmen who presumably aren't interested in art. They would have had a different tune to sing for a more general audience. But the ugly truth about television is that the "quality" of television programing has nothing to do with its "success." In fact, "quality" may be not merely irrelevant but a distraction.

A labor-relations negotiator for one of the major television networks pointed out that a survey of TV audiences revealed that it did not matter which writer wrote any particular episode of a TV dramatic series. The quality of one writer's contribution over another had no demonstrable effect upon the show's rating. It was said without malice, and accepted without regret, by the writer-members of the negotiating team which faced him across the table.

Balzac might have wept; Dickens might have grown white with rage, and Hemingway might have punched him in the face. TV writers are a tougher breed. They pressed their lips together and pushed on to more pragmatic matters, determined to squeeze from their cut-rate Medicis the best price they could get for their creative agony and ecstasy.

"Success," as you may have guessed, lies in the amounts of money which are returned to networks, producers, actors, advertising agencies and so on. As long as these figures keep going up (and they have, without interruption, since 1948), then television is a success by every measurable criterion which can be applied. Dollars and cents can be added up; numbers of sets can be added up; numbers of viewers can be added up; sales in stores can be added up. Television works. It makes money. Money for everyone remotely connected with it, from girls who sit on assembly lines and spot-weld electrical connections to some of the largest corporations in America.

Procter & Gamble, which spends a staggering 167 million dollars annually on advertising, spends 148.8 million dollars of it in television—about 89 per cent of its annual budget. Hershey Chocolate, on the other hand, has never advertised any place but on the wrappers of its candy bars. There are corporate fanatics at both extremes of the spectrum. The corporations which regularly spend in the neighborhood of 90 percent of their advertising budget on TV include Gillette (94.2 percent), Block Drug Co. (91.1 percent), J. B. Williams (95.8 percent). The champion appears to be the Consolidated Cigar Company (Muriels and Dutch Masters), which spends a flat 98 percent of its 10.53 million dollar budget on TV.

Businessmen don't kid themselves. TV works. It works spectacularly. Lincoln Steffens said of Russia once, "I have seen the future and it works." He could only have meant: "I have seen the future and it is in operation." America is not merely in operation; it is in a state of a permanent explosion, and television is probably the most dramatic portion of that growth explosion.

It is this explosion, in fact, which angers and annoys intellectuals. Much of the current dissatisfaction with television derives from the intellectuals' hatred of it. As a class, those who watch it the least hate it the most. This isn't a simple "Well of course" statement, because there

are those who watch it a great deal and despise it because
they have been told that it is fashionable to despise it.
Stretch them out on the psychiatrist's couch and they will
whisper, "I like it, but I shouldn't."

The whispering campaign against TV is remorseless and
bitter and it started, oddly enough, when TV actually did
have a chance of becoming a new art form. Intellectuals
hated it when it first flickered on the home screen. They
sneered at it when it was in its "golden age," when Paddy
Chayefsky and Horton Foote and Robert Alan Aurthur
were doing some of their best work. They denigrated it
when it had its greatest freedom and was showing its best
promise, as in *Playhouse 90*.

Their sneering, I feel, helped to dry up its early chances.
Now the medium has grown immensely and vulgarly and
all of the numbers have doubled, quadrupled and the
business is largely an expression of cost accounting, and
the intellectual establishment is infuriated that it has not
disappeared. Their comments about its quality are more
justified today than they ever were, but their influence
has diminished.

There has been greater notice taken of Newton Minow's
declaration that television was a "wasteland" than ever
greeted T. S. Eliot's first creation of the image. Intellectuals are fascists when it comes to matters of public
taste, and they hoped that once the chairman of the
F.C.C. declared television was a wasteland it would be
taken away from the private entrepreneurs and turned
over to a Federal art commission. Since my own faith in
Federal art commissions is a little weaker than it is in
Lew Wasserman and MCA, I am not so sure that television
would do any better in the hands of civil servants than it
is currently doing. I do know that I can now criticize it
without worrying about having the F.B.I. look me over.
The emotional anger which lies at the heart of most intellectuals when they think about television is not its lack
of quality, but its booming, bouncing, vigorous success. It
is a dungheap on American civilization which grows
larger, and look at all the fleas it attracts!

An intellectual writer in *The New Republic* once observed that he found programs like *The Defenders* of-
fensively pretentious and rather preferred the occasional

dramaturgy and the performances on *Wagon Train*. By way of showing the contrast, he opposed a story line of *The Defenders* against another on *Wagon Train*. *Wagon Train* came off better.

The New Republic may know whereof it speaks when it talks about world issues and foreign policy. But television is my occupation and I have spent years in it and I know more about its ins and outs than the editors of *The New Republic* know about Vietnam. The "intent" of *The Defenders* was always a serious one and the "intent" of *Wagon Train* was to slice 52 minutes of dramatic salami. TV, which is swamped with base intentions, needs good intentions more than anything else. It surely does not need critics who deprecate its good intentions and salute the salami. The producers of *Wagon Train* need not congratulate themselves on his praise because it is the sneering praise of a man who thinks them whores, and as whores finds them rather becoming. Intellectuals rejected TV when it waddled, and their influence could have nurtured it. Now it marches like a jack-booted army. Who needs them now?

Is television as bad as intellectuals claim it is? If so, why? Can it ever get any better?

To begin with the first question—television is no worse, in content or execution, than much of the content of other popular entertainment media. I will match the lousiest TV show with the shoddiest movie Hollywood ever turned out and both of them with the most miserable play which ever opened on Broadway and all of them with the sleaziest book ever published by a reputable trade-book publisher. I hereby offer two tickets to *The Jackie Gleason Show* to any critic, pundit, esthete, or Renaissance figure who can demonstrate to me the difference in cultural "worth" between *Gilligan's Island*, *The Yellow Rolls Royce* (written by Terence Rattigan and starring every million-dollar motion-picture star in Christendom), *Barefoot in the Park* (directed by Mike Nichols), and *Candy* (originally published as pornography by Maurice Girodias and later readvertised as "satire"). Each of them was conceived for the same purpose—to turn a dollar. Each succeeded. Which of them adds a cubit to the stature of mankind?

And yet there were television shows which have moved us and shaken us. Have people forgotten *Days of Wine and Roses* by J. P. Miller? William Gibson's play, *The Miracle Worker* was originally a television show. *Marty* was originally a television play. Rod Serling's *Patterns* was a better TV show than it was a movie, as was Abby Mann's *Judgment at Nuremberg.*

Have the Russians forgotten *The Plot to Kill Stalin?* Did the intellectuals get rid of Joe McCarthy or was it television? Was Hollywood's film of John F. Kennedy's life a more tasteful tribute to his memory than the Robert Saudek series, *Profiles in Courage?* Has the celebrated guardianship of the dramatic form by Lincoln Center come up with productions which equaled Henry Weinstein's productions of *Play of the Week?*

Sholom Aleichem was done better on TV than he is being done in *Fiddler on the Roof.* Was Jack Gilford given as rich an opportunity to express his comic genius as an actor on Broadway when he was in *A Funny Thing Happened on the Way to the Forum* as he was given when he played the little old Jewish winemaker on *The 700-Year-Old Gang* on TV?

There is so *much* of TV that it would be manic to protest that so much of it is bad. Where there is a plethora of anything, it is almost axiomatic that most of it will be terrible. Television gets blamed for its high visibility. There it is, under the switch of your set, almost 20 hours a day, to confirm your worst feelings about the state of American culture. *What's My Line?* is there every Sunday night to remind you that the Russians are not going to have much of a task burying us—if television is the way they choose to do it.

Why is so much of it bad? Because it is so successful. It sells products, it makes stars, it enriches ex-mailroom boys. Because the numbers add up. Those awful incomprehensible numbers. You may hate *Perry Mason,* but it is reputedly General Franco's favorite American television show. It is also the favorite of a little old Jewish lady in Santa Monica, who told me why she preferred it to *The Defenders.* "I always know, from *Perry Mason,* who did it," she said. "From *The Defenders* you never know who's guilty."

I think she's got a point. People want to know who the bad guys are.

Why is TV so bad and still so successful? Because American taste—and the taste of the English, French, Germans and other vidiots—is awful. Lincoln is reputed to have remarked that God must have loved the common people, since He made so many of them. Lincoln must have made the remark when he was speaking as a politician. Politicians adore the common man and so does Procter & Gamble. The commoner, the better. The saddening truth about television is that the audience is out there, listening, watching, in numbers which shake us and they haven't reached out to turn off the sets. They switch channels and the networks are as sensitive to the clicking of those switches as they are to the very air they breathe. But the sets stay on. More and more of them.

And now they will be watching in color and every pilot film being shot today on Hollywood sound stages for the next season is being shot in color. No one wants to lose the audience with color sets. They won't watch anything which isn't shown in color. It won't matter whether a show in black and white is better. If it's not in color, they won't watch it.

Technicolor motion pictures are commanding enormous prices for television showing. Enormous? Well, 1 million dollars each for two hours. Such prices occur because the number of pictures in color is limited. It is this limitation of "product" which has given rise to a recently announced partnership plan by the networks and the Hollywood studios to produce motion pictures for television on budgets of 500,000 to 1,500,000 dollars each. According to reports, they would be shown principally in theaters abroad, but in this country would be designed to fill television's need for full-length motion pictures. The economics appear to make sense. The esthetics appear to be imperiled.

Why would a network spend 1,000,000 dollars to make a movie for two showings on different evenings? By now you realize that 1,000,000 dollars isn't much. A two-hour film shown in prime time (which is 8 P.M. to 11 P.M.) brings the cost of each showing down to 500,000 dollars, or 250,000 dollars an hour. Is 250,000 dollars a lot of money for one hour of TV? It depends. The Chrysler Theater costs 150,000 dollars an hour each week it is shown. When Bob Hope appears on the show, the cost soars to 400,000 dollars for an hour. Does the show improve 250,000 dollars with Bob Hope on it? Someone thinks so. The Chrysler Corporation, presumably. They've got to sell a lot of Plymouths and Dodges to make that money back. But people not only watch Hope and laugh at his jokes; they also buy Chrysler Corporation cars. Are the same people laughing and buying? That's what the advertising business is all about. Maybe the whole thing is a Madison Avenue bubble and it will burst. But it has been going on for more than fifteen years and the bubble is getting bigger.

Can television get any better? In some strangely unnoticed ways it is getting better. The commercials are getting better. They are more interesting. They are using techniques of *cinema vérité*, their music is better, and they are getting much more sophisticated than in the days of George Washington Hill and his motto of "Hit 'em over the head and do it again and again and again."

I sometimes think the commercials are more interesting than the shows they separate and interrupt. There is a famous, and probably apocryphal, story that a television program was turned down by advertisers on the grounds that it was so good and so absorbing that interruption of it for commercial messages would have, in the view of the advertising agency, built up viewer resentment and resistance to the product. In brief, the show was simply too good to be interrupted.

I don't believe the story because I don't believe in the sensitivity of the huckster. I have met a lot of hucksters over the years and while I found many of them charming and witty and urbane and intelligent, not one of them had enough sensitivity to dampen a Kleenex. They have made their commercials better and Hollywood has cooperated by making the shows worse.

If, like the little old lady in Santa Monica, you want to know who the bad guys are—who is the villain and who is guilty—why not start blaming ourselves? I mean you and me as television viewers. We look at the idiot tube, according to A. C. Nielsen, on an *average* of five hours and twenty-five minutes a day. I know that you only look at it once a week, or only at the 11-o'clock news, but think of the people who are watching it eight hours a day to bring up your low-level viewing.

We've got to stop. We simply have to reach over and snap the switch off and leave it off. By the hundreds, by the thousands, by the hundreds of thousands and by the millions. Then there will be panic. Panic on Sixth Avenue. Panic on Madison Avenue. Panic in the Valley. Panic in Beverly Hills. Panic in Brentwood and Bel Air. Panic at Desilu-Gower, Desilu-Culver. Panic at Warner's. Panic at Fox.

A. C. Nielsen will be up on the carpet. Heads will roll. Checks will flutter. Seers will be brought in. Pundits will be summoned. Books will be written. Songs will be sung. Birds will fly and the sun will shine again. The voices of children will be heard in the streets. Card games will be played. People will lose weight and admire one another. Lovers will get back to the couch in the living room.

Fred Allen will come down Allen's Alley again. Lum and Abner will return. Artie Shaw will go back to the clarinet. TV dinners will vanish. Repairmen will fix radios and clocks again. Nothing will be made of plastic.

That's the best that could happen. The next best thing would be for God to appear and speak in Lew Wasserman's ear and say: "Make 'A' pictures for TV." And I think He will. For my mother was never so smart as when she said the rich were just smarter sooner.

The Fine Edge
of Awareness

by Russell Lynes

A magazine editor reminds the individual that a true appreciation of art depends upon his own response, not on what he is told he should like by others. Lip service does not constitute genuine appreciation.

Last summer, several months before the much disputed Solomon R. Guggenheim Museum, designed by Frank Lloyd Wright, was opened in New York City, I was walking past it when I was approached by a young man. He wore a sport shirt hanging outside his trousers, and he spoke with a strong Spanish accent.

"Mister," he said, "what's that building?"

I said that it was a new museum, a picture gallery.

He looked up for a moment at its expanding spiral walls with their deeply cut shadows and unfamiliar contours.

"It's very beautiful," he said. After a pause, he added, "It must have cost a lot of money."

It was a simple statement of enthusiasm and wonder, and it has stuck in my mind. This I thought, was honest appreciation of the art of architecture. The young man was not put off by the unfamiliar and the unconventional, and yet he was impressed, as most of us are, by an unmistakable richness in what he saw. He was using his senses and not his prejudices, something a great deal harder to do than most of us think.

It seems to me that when we approach the arts we are all too likely to be self-conscious and on the defensive, forgetting that it is they that are trying to please us and not we who are trying to please them. There is nothing we can do to a work of art by either ignoring it or glaring at it, but there is a great deal it would like to do for us if we would give it half a chance. Art does not set out to be mysterious but, rather, to reveal mysteries; it does not seek to lock doors against us but to open them. We are likely to think that to appreciate the arts we must carry a pocketful of keys and a headful of historical knowledge. The trouble with this is that no matter how many keys we may carry the one we need is as likely as not to be missing, and historical knowledge, while it can enhance one's pleasure in the arts, cannot initiate it.

Pleasure—or appreciation, if you prefer—of any sort is a combination of discovery and receptiveness, and one is not likely to discover any pleasure unless he is in a mood to receive it. To feel the sensation of pleasure that the arts can give, whether in music or painting or architecture or sculpture, requires not just a conscientious effort of the mind but a certain sandpapering of the senses. You don't, for example, learn how to look at pictures by reading books about them. You learn to look at pictures by looking at them, by exercising the muscles of the sense of sight.

This, I grant you, sounds like a mightily mixed metaphor—and it is. But delight in the art is a mightily mixed bag of experiences, of emotions, of senses that anyone can have who wants them. Let me try to explain with an experience of my own.

About a year ago I found myself engaged in an enterprise that I strongly suspected was none of my business. On the seventh floor of a New York warehouse, several thousand pieces of modern glass of every description from almost every part of the world were set out on long tables and packing cases and benches—an astonishing variety of colors and textures and shapes. Along with four other persons—a museum director, an architect, a design consultant, and a famous craftsman—I was to select from the delightful confusion an even hundred pieces that in my estimation should be included in an exhibition to be shown in several other museums across the country.

My official qualifications for being a juror of such an exhibition were not only dubious, they were nonexistent. I know a great deal less about glass than any housewife who has to replace broken tumblers. Why, for heaven's sake, had I let myself be caught in this situation?

I needn't have worried, though I confess I was tempted to steal away when I saw the choices that faced me. After carefully examining a few of the pieces that were displayed for us on specially lighted tables, I discovered that to pick and choose demanded no special knowledge of glass, of the techniques of making and shaping it, or of its history. It demanded only that I exercise the very same judgment I had learned from years of looking at painting and sculpture and architecture. I do not consider my eyes infallible —far from it—but they have been trained to look hard at objects, to see them in the context of their time, and to judge them in relation to their purpose, the materials of which they are made, and the intention of their makers.

There is nothing mysterious about glass, I discovered. It is merely a material, like paint or stone or bronze, out of which other kinds of objects of art, at which I am used to looking, are made. But there is no question that there is something extremely mysterious about the human eye. It may be totally blind in an art gallery and as sensitive as a barometer at a glove counter. It may communicate only boredom in front of a Rembrandt portrait but a sensation of wonder in front of a sunset. The eye, in other words, sees what it has trained itself to look at and look for, and it rejects what fails to arouse its curiosity or excite its respect. It can be timid, or it can be adventurous. It can limit experience to the familiar and the safe, or it can constantly search for new experiences, new sensations, and new kinds of pleasure.

Unfortunately, there are a great many people who never learn to make their eyes work for them—or their ears, either, for that matter—beyond the most practical, everyday uses. But more women use their eyes for pleasure than do men, and this has been true in America for a long time. In our country, decisions of visual taste traditionally have been left to women. It is they who have decided what the house shall look like inside and out; choices that determine the looks and feel and atmosphere of the home, an art in itself. But further than that, the American woman traditionally has been responsible for the cultural atmosphere in which her children have been brought up, including education and what used to be called the "refinements"—the arts and niceties of civilized living. Men, it has been assumed, were far too busy cultivating business or the soil to have time to cultivate the arts.

If you have the habit, as I have, of reading what visitors to America think about our society, you have already discovered that in the last century they were likely to find our women a great deal better company than our men. Men, it seems, were always taking themselves off to their counting houses either to do business or to talk about it, while women found time to read, to listen to music and perform it, to cultivate the arts in a variety of ways. You will discover, indeed, that much of the very best criticism of architecture in the last century was written by women, and behind every movement to interest the public in the arts there was a phalanx of devoted women pressing their husbands to do their cultural duty.

An Englishman named James Silk Buckingham, who visited here in the 1830's, found American women not only "much handsomer than the men" and "almost uniformly good-looking" with a "more than usual degree of feminine delicacy," but in their conversation "always equal to the men, and often superior to them in the extent of their reading and in the shrewdness of their observations." About eighty years later, Henry Adams, looking back over his life, said quite flatly that "the American woman of the nineteenth century was much better company than the American man."

Whether Mr. Buckingham and Mr. Adams would find this cultural superiority of women today I do not know, but I do know that the arts now reach—as they did not a century ago—into just about every nook and cranny of the country.

It is no longer considered sissyish for men to be interested in painting and music, and the old cartoon that showed the husband sleeping through an opera to which his wife had dragged him is as flavorless as yesterday's coffee. The arts have become a family matter, and the demand for them has increased as our leisure has increased. Twenty-five years ago we had 600 museums in America; now we have 2,500. We have some 2,300 communities with civic theater groups, and there are 30 major symphony orchestras and 650 professional and semiprofessional orchestras, not including those in schools or colleges. As

Jacques Barzun has observed, America is having a love affair with culture.

But I am afraid that statistics like these can be sadly misleading. It is easy to say that the arts are flourishing because three million people a year go through the turnstiles of New York City's Metropolitan Museum of Art, and because on an ordinary Sunday 30,000 people wander through its galleries. But the health of the arts cannot be measured in numbers; it can be measured only in the satisfaction they give. Unquestionably a great deal of what passes for genuine interest in the arts is actually no more than lip service. There are a great many people who go to museums and concerts and to the opera and serious theater only because they feel they ought to or because it is the thing to do—not because they cannot stay away. Something unquestionably rubs off on everyone who goes, however unwillingly; but not much rubs off on a snob, and unfortunately it's only for snobbish reasons that a great many people make a show of being interested in the arts. They are not keeping up with any basic needs of the spirit; they are merely keeping up with the Joneses.

I imagine that the percentage of intellectual snobs is about constant and that there was a comparable number of them in the last century. But there are also a great many people, named Jones or Smith or Johnson, to whom the arts provide a kind of satisfaction that those who try to ape their gestures and repeat their opinions cannot understand. Theirs is not a love affair with culture with a capital "C" but a warm and devoted friendship with one of the arts.

I do not know anyone deriving real satisfaction from painting or music or reading who fell in love with them at first sight. I don't know anyone who enjoys the arts but is afraid of them—afraid of not knowing enough, afraid of being fooled, afraid of misunderstanding, afraid of being bored—any more than one is afraid of one's friends. One gets to know the arts by being in their company, and, as in friendship, pleasure in the arts increases with time. Just as one singles out the friends he wants to spend a great deal of time with, so he singles out the arts he most enjoys. It is as ridiculous to say, "I like art" as it is to

like everyone I meet." It is also as ridiculous to
ze the arts you do not like on first meeting as it is
iticize someone you have seen only across a crowded
room.

But let me carry this analogy one step farther by trying
to answer the question: How does one become friends with
the arts?

As I said earlier, it is the arts that are trying to please
us and not we who are trying to please them. But they
cannot please us unless we make a gesture in their direction, as the women of the nineteenth century did. No
work of art can pour out its soul to you all at once, any
more than a friend can. It requires not only your un-
divided attention but your willingness to sit and look or
listen—and beyond that it requires that you understand
its language.

The language of painting may be as unfamiliar to you as
an African dialect and though you may be drawn to it
by its superficial appearance, as one frequently is to people whose language one cannot understand, you will not
know what it is trying to say to you until you learn its
vocabulary. There is no better way to learn any language
than by being continually exposed to it. So it is with the
language of the arts; you do not have to be fluent in their
language to enjoy their friendship, but the more fluent
you become, the greater your pleasure will be.

It was this that was brought so forcefully home to me
the day I was trying to judge the glass for the exhibition.
As the day progressed, I understood better and better the
language of the glass, its shades of meaning, its subtleties,
its intentions. It was trying to please me, and I was eager
to be pleased, and by the end of the day we were acquain-
tances. If I go on looking at glass over the years, eventually we will become good friends, with respect for each
other's judgment. The burden rests on me. I have to keep
at it.

But my way of becoming friends with the arts may not
be your way. Each individual arrives at the satisfactions
the arts can give him, if he ever does, by a process all his
own. The process must start with curiosity—the kind of
curiosity that prompted the young man to ask me about
the Guggenheim Museum. This sort leads to exploration.

Inevitably, exploration will lead to discovery of a world as wide as the limitless mind of man, as tall as his aspirations, and as deep as his despair.

The world of the arts is by no means always comfortable, but neither is it likely ever to be boring. It is full of surprises, humor, traps for the unwary, and challenges to smugness. It is a world of moods as well as of revelations, of beliefs and fears, of unpleasant truth as well as of delicious fantasy. Perhaps it is arrogant to say that anyone who does not venture into this world is only half-interested in life. I say it, nonetheless.

How Do You Know
It's Good?

by Marya Mannes

A social critic attacks the false standards by which so much art is judged, decries the American tendency to prefer something simply because of its newness, and proposes as the only valid judgment for all the arts the absolute response of the individual.

Suppose there were no critics to tell us how to react to a picture, a play, or a new composition of music. Suppose we wandered innocent as the dawn into an art exhibition of unsigned paintings. By what standards, by what values would we decide whether they were good or bad, talented or untalented, successes or failures? How can we ever know that what we think is right?

For the last fifteen or twenty years the fashion in criticism or appreciation of the arts has been to deny the existence of any valid criteria and to make the words "good" or "bad" irrelevant, immaterial, and inapplicable. There is no such thing, we are told, as a set of standards, first acquired through experience and knowledge and later imposed on the subject under discussion. This has been a popular approach, for it relieves the critic of the responsibility of judgment and the public of the necessity of knowledge. It pleases those resentful of disciplines, it flatters the empty-minded by calling them open-minded, it comforts the confused. Under the banner of democracy and the kind of equality which our forefathers did *not* mean, it says, in effect, "Who are you to tell us what is good or bad?" This is the same cry used so long and so effectively by the producers of mass media who insist that it is the public, not they, who decides what it wants to hear and see, and that for a critic to say that *this* program **is** bad and *this* program is good is purely a reflection of personal taste. Nobody recently has expressed this philosophy more succinctly than Dr. Frank Stanton, the highly intelligent president of CBS television. At a hearing before the Federal Communications Commission, this phrase escaped him under questioning: "One man's mediocrity is another man's good program."

There is no better way of saying, "No values are absolute." There is another important aspect to this philosophy of *laissez-faire:* It is the fear, in all observers of all forms of art, of guessing wrong. This fear is well come by, for who has not heard of the contemporary outcries against artists who later were called great? Every age has its arbiters who do not grow with their times, who cannot tell evolution from revolution or the difference between frivolous faddism, amateurish experimentation, and profound and necessary change. Who wants to be caught *flagrante delicto* with an error of judgment as serious as this? It is far safer, and certainly easier, to look at a picture or a play or a poem and to say, "This is hard to understand, but it may be good," or simply to welcome it as a new form. The word "new"—in our country especially—has magical connotations. What is new must be good; what is old is probably bad. And if a critic can describe the new in language that nobody can understand, he's safer still. If he has mastered the art of saying nothing with exquisite complexity, nobody can quote him later as saying anything.

But all these, I maintain, are forms of abdication from the responsibility of judgment. In creating, the artist commits himself; in appreciating, you have a commitment of your own. For after all, it is the audience which makes the arts. A climate of appreciation is essential to its flowering, and the higher the expectations of the public, the better the performance of the artist. Conversely, only a public ill-served by its critics could have accepted as art and as literature so much in these last years that has been neither. If anything goes, everything goes; and at the bottom of the junkpile lie the discarded standards too.

But what are these standards? How do you get them? How do you know they're the right ones? How can you make a clear pattern out of so many intangibles, including that greatest one, the very private I?

Well for one thing, it's fairly obvious that the more you read and see and hear, the more equipped you'll be to practice that art of association which is at the basis of all understanding and judgment. The more you live and the more you look, the more aware you are of a consistent pattern—as universal as the stars, as the tides, as breathing, as night and day—underlying everything. I would call this pattern and this rhythm an order. Not order—*an* order. Within it exists an incredible diversity of forms. Without it lies chaos. I would further call this order—this incredible diversity held within one pattern—health. And I would call chaos—the wild cells of destruction—sickness. It is in the end up to you to distinguish between the diversity that is health and the chaos that is sickness, and you can't do this without a process of association that can link a bar of Mozart with the corner of a Vermeer painting, or a Stravinsky score with a Picasso abstraction; or that can relate an aggressive act with a Franz Kline painting and a fit of coughing with a John Cage composition.

There is no accident in the fact that certain expressions of art live for all time and that others die with the moment, and although you may not always define the reasons, you can ask the questions. What does an artist say that is timeless; how does he say it? How much is fashion, how much is merely reflection? Why is Sir Walter Scott so hard to read now, and Jane Austen not? Why is baroque right for one age and too effulgent for another?

Can a standard of craftsmanship apply to art of all ages, or does each have its own, and different, definitions? You may have been aware, inadvertently, that craftsmanship has become a dirty word these years because, again, it implies standards—something done well or done badly. The result of this convenient avoidance is a plenitude of actors who can't project their voices, singers who can't phrase their songs, poets who can't communicate emotion, and writers who have no vocabulary—not to speak of painters who can't draw. The dogma now is that craftsmanship gets in the way of expression. You can do better if you don't know *how* you do it, let alone *what* you're doing.

I think it is time you helped reverse this trend by trying to rediscover craft: the command of the chosen instrument, whether it is a brush, a word, or a voice. When you begin to detect the difference between freedom and sloppiness, between serious experimentation and ego-therapy, between skill and slickness, between strength and violence, you are on your way to separating the sheep from the goats, a form of segregation denied us for quite a while. All you need to restore it is a small bundle of standards and a Geiger counter that detects fraud, and we might begin our tour of the arts in an area where both are urgently needed: contemporary painting.

I don't know what's worse: to have to look at acres of bad art to find the little good, or to read what the critics say about it all. In no other field of expression has so much double-talk flourished, so much confusion prevailed, and so much nonsense been circulated: further evidence of the close interdependence between the arts and the critical climate they inhabit. It will be my pleasure to share with you some of this double-talk so typical of our times.

Item one: preface for a catalogue of an abstract painter:

"Time-bound meditation experiencing a life; sincere with plastic piety at the threshold of hallowed arcana; a striving for pure ideation giving shape to inner drive; formalized patterns where neural balances reach a fiction." End of quote. Know what this artist paints like now?

Item two: a review in the *Art News:*

". . . a weird and disparate assortment of material, but the monstrosity which bloomed into his most recent cancer of aggregations is present in some form everywhere. . . ." Then, later, "A gluttony of things and processes terminated by a glorious constipation."

Item three, same magazine, review of an artist who welds automobile fragments into abstract shapes:

"Each fragment . . . is made an extreme of human exasperation, torn at and fought all the way, and has its rightness of form as if by accident. *Any technique that requires order or discipline would just be the human ego.* No, these must be egoless, uncontrolled, undesigned and different enough to give you a bang—fifty miles an hour around a telephone pole. . . ."

"Any technique that requires order of discipline would just be the human ego." What does he mean—"just be"?

What are they really talking about? Is this journalism? Is it criticism? Or is it that other convenient abdication from standards of performance and judgment practiced by so many artists and critics that they, like certain writers who deal only in sickness and depravity, "reflect the chaos about them"? Again, whose chaos? Whose depravity?

I had always thought that the prime function of art was to create order *out* of chaos—again, not the order of neatness or rigidity or convention or artifice, but the order of clarity by which one will and one vision could draw the essential truth out of apparent confusion. I still do. It is not enough to use parts of a car to convey the brutality of the machine. This is as slavishly representative, and just as easy, as arranging dried flowers under glass to convey nature.

Speaking of which, i.e., the use of real materials (burlap, old gloves, bottletops) in lieu of pigment, this is what one critic had to say about an exhibition of Assemblage at the Museum of Modern Art last year:

> Spotted throughout the show are indisputable works of art, accounting for a quarter or even a half of the total display. But the remainder are works of non-art, anti-art, and art substitutes that are the aesthetic counterparts of the social deficiencies that land people in the clink on charges of vagrancy. These aesthetic bankrupts . . . have no legitimate ideological roof over their heads and not the price of a square intellectual meal, much less a spiritual sandwich, in their pockets.

I quote these words of John Canaday of *The New York Times* as an example of the kind of criticism which puts responsibility to an intelligent public above popularity with an intellectual coterie. Canaday has the courage to say what he thinks and the capacity to say it clearly: two qualities notably absent from his profession.

Next to art, I would say that appreciation and evaluation in the field of music is the most difficult. For it is rarely possible to judge a new composition at one hearing only. What seems confusing or fragmented at first might well become clear and organic a third time. Or it might not. The only salvation here for the listener is, again, an instinct born of experience and association which allows him to separate intent from accident, design from experimentation, and pretense from conviction. Much of contemporary music is, like its sister art, merely a reflection of the composer's own fragmentation: an absorption in self and symbols at the expense of communication with others. The artist, in short, says to the public: If you don't understand this, it's because you're dumb. I maintain that you are not. You may have to go part way or even halfway to meet the artist, but if you must go the whole way, it's his fault, not yours. Hold fast to that. And remember it too when you read new poetry, that estranged sister of music.

> A multitude of causes, unknown to former times, are now acting with a combined force to blunt the discriminating powers of the mind, and, unfitting it for all voluntary exertion, to reduce it to a state of almost savage torpor. The most effective of these causes are the great national events which are daily taking place and the increasing accumulation of men in cities, where the uniformity of their occupations produces a craving for extraordinary incident, which the rapid communication of intelligence hourly gratifies. To this tendency of life and manners, the literature and theatrical exhibitions of the country have conformed themselves.

This startlingly applicable comment was written in the year 1800 by William Wordsworth in the preface to his *Lyrical Ballads;* and it has been cited by Edwin Muir in his recently published book, *The Estate of Poetry*. Muir states that poetry's effective range and influence have diminished alarmingly in the modern world. He believes in the inherent and indestructible qualities of the human mind and the great and permanent objects that act upon it, and suggests that the audience will increase when "poetry loses what obscurity is left in it by attempting greater themes, for great themes have to be stated clearly." If you keep that firmly in mind and resist, in Muir's words, "the vast dissemination of secondary objects that isolate us from the natural world," you have gone a long way toward equipping yourself for the examination of any work of art.

When you come to theatre, in this extremely hasty tour of the arts, you can approach it on two different levels. You can bring to it anticipation and innocence, giving yourself up, as it were, to the life on the stage and reacting to it emotionally, if the play is good, or listlessly, if the play is boring; a part of the audience organism that expresses its favor by silence or laughter and its disfavor by coughing and rustling. Or you can bring to it certain critical faculties that may heighten, rather than diminish, your enjoyment.

You can ask yourselves whether the actors are truly in their parts or merely projecting themselves; whether the scenery helps or hurts the mood; whether the playwright is honest with himself, his characters, and you. Somewhere along the line you can learn to distinguish between the true creative act and the false arbitrary gesture; between fresh observation and stale cliché; between the avant-garde play that is pretentious drivel and the avant-garde play that finds new ways to say old truths.

Purpose and craftsmanship—end and means—these are the keys to your judgment in all the arts. What is this painter trying to say when he slashes a broad band of black across a white canvas and lets the edges dribble down? Is it a statement of violence? Is it a self-portrait? If it is *one* of these, has he made you believe it? Or is this a gesture of the ego or a form of therapy? If it shocks you, what does it shock you into?

And what of this tight little painting of bright flowers in a vase? Is the painter saying anything new about flowers? Is it different from a million other canvases of flowers? Has it any life, any meaning, beyond its statement? Is there any pleasure in its forms or texture? The question is not whether a thing is abstract or representational, whether it is "modern" or conventional. The question, inexorably, is whether it is good. And this is a decision which only you, on the basis of instinct, experience, and association, can make for yourself. It takes independence and courage. It involves, moreover, the risk of wrong decision and the humility, after the passage of time, of recognizing it as such. As we grow and change and learn, our attitudes can change too, and what we once thought obscure or "difficult" can later emerge as coherent and illuminating. Entrenched prejudices, obdurate opinions are as sterile as no opinions at all.

Yet standards there are, timeless as the universe itself. And when you have committed yourself to them, you have acquired a passport to that elusive but immutable realm of truth. Keep it with you in the forests of bewilderment. And never be afraid to speak up.

Surviving
Through
Science

Can Science Prevent War?

by Arthur Larson

The director of the World Rule of Law Center at Duke University suggests that, though science can be a Frankenstein's monster capable of destruction, the scientific method can be a positive way of preserving peace among creative societies.

In physical science man has to an impressive degree learned to control and direct the forces and materials supplied by nature, for better or for worse. In human affairs he has not.

The reason is that man has seldom applied to the conduct of human affairs even the most elementary techniques that he has used for generations in discovering facts and putting them to work in the physical sciences.

There are three ways to approach knowledge: scientific, nonscientific, and pseudoscientific.

The scientific approach begins with finding the facts through direct examination and experiment, and then applying to these facts tested methods of analysis and verification.

The nonscientific approach merely reacts blindly to the environment, guided by nothing but instincts, emotions, prejudices, and superstitions.

The pseudoscientific approach borrows the trappings of the scientific, including elaborate paraphernalia, complex demonstrations, and polysyllabic terminologies, but suffers from two oversights: failure to get the facts in the first place, and failure to test results against reality.

The tragedy of man's attempt to bring order into his political and social relations is that this attempt has floundered between the nonscientific and the pseudoscientific without ever coming to rest on the scientific.

Before the Age of Science, if you wanted to find out what the inside of the human body was like, you did not open a human body; you opened Aristotle. When Galileo, to test whether the speed of falling objects increased with their weight, dropped two balls of differing weights from the Leaning Tower of Pisa instead of accepting the answer contained in the books, it was considered a piece of impertinence. Today this fact seems almost unbelievable— yet for the most part our conduct of political and international affairs is still dominated by pre-Galileo methods.

World wars have been started with what seems to have been less real investigation of the facts bearing on the probable outcome than a scientist would put into the dietary habits of an obscure insect. How much research did the Kaiser conduct to support his conviction that the British would never enter World War I, not to mention the United States? With this lesson of history behind him, Hitler nevertheless made precisely the same error of fact, with similar results.

Similarly, millions of Soviet citizens have repeatedly been brought to the verge of starvation because of slavish adherence to doctrinaire ideology rather than reliance on observable facts on how to get crops and livestock produced. The Communists display the most grandiose example of the pseudoscientific approach to human affairs in history. Their jargon is shot through with appeals to the scientific method, but their starting point is *a priori* dogma. Their gaze is still riveted on a state of facts dated 1850. They are fighting a kind of raw capitalism that may or may not have existed a century ago, but certainly does not exist now. Their pure ideology presupposes a species of human creature with motivations that direct observation would quickly show do not exist except in rare cases.

By contrast, the United States has at times seemed to symbolize the nonscientific approach—a kind of assumption that if everyone just does what comes naturally, the good life for all will somehow emerge. This view is typified by the economics of Adam Smith, and, indeed, the lusty surge of industrial development in the Western world owes much to the drives engendered by this attitude. One of the products of this experience is the fragment of phony American folklore that teaches that our society came into being as unself-consciously as the unfolding of the petals of a flower, and that although in personal and business life planning is the key to success, in public life planning is un-American and unqualifiedly, evil. Even now, many politicians think that the most devastating insult you can apply to an opponent is to call him a "planner." This attitude was no doubt reenforced by the fact that, in the thirties, planning came to be associated with Communism and socialism. Other sweeping ideas to change society such as technology came under the same cloud.

The true fact is that at certain key points in our history Americans have applied the genuine scientific approach by first studying the facts, then conceiving a definite design and building toward it.

The outstanding example is our Constitution—the product of a gigantic effort of intellectual research and creativity.

When the great farmlands of the Midwest opened up, Americans concluded that the West was going to be a country of small-family farms. The result was the Homestead Act, a concept of breathtaking scope and imagination, which methodically translated this blueprint into reality.

In somewhat the same way, although the persistence of *laissez-faire* thought permitted the growth of the cartel system in Europe, Americans looked at the facts rather than the pages of Adam Smith and saw that the end result of supposedly perfect competition was all too often the death of competition. They deliberately decided that the American economy was to be nonmonopolistic. Accordingly, they passed the Sherman Anti-Trust Act, the Clayton Act, and the Norris-LaGuardia Act.

Again, Americans perceived that the bargaining power of organized labor was not equal to that of employers, and therefore set out to try to make it at least approximately so by devising and subsequently revising the Wagner Labor Relations Act.

On the international scene, after World War II, the facts showed that everyone's peace and welfare depended on economic and technical rebuilding and development, first by the devastated countries of Europe, and then by the underdeveloped countries of Asia, Africa, and Latin

America. The magnificent concept of economic and technical aid was the deliberately designed result.

The area outside the physical sciences where the authentic scientific approach has been most successfully applied is that of economics, particularly in the prevention of severe recessions and in the reconciling of free enterprise with orderly growth through careful observation of an array of "economic indicators" and skilful manipulation of such controls as discount rates, taxes, government purchase policy, social insurance, and fiscal measures.

Of all areas in which the need to control events rather than be controlled by them is urgent, that of international relations should have the highest priority.

How well are we doing in applying the power of intelligence to this task? The answer is that, until recently, it never seems to have occurred to the world's leaders that the techniques of intellectual research had anything to contribute to solving the problem of war between nations.

A rational approach to any problem begins with getting the facts—facts which are accurate and current. International relations today are being conducted on the basis of facts that are from eighteen to 300 years out of date.

A partial checklist of current misconcepts of fact bearing on the ultimate issue of war and peace may serve to support this statement.

The first misconcept is that diplomacy is the only valid method of settling international disputes. The fact is that old-fashioned power-politics diplomacy is virtually obsolete as a method of settling major disputes. Since it still remains almost the only technique used in international relations, we can begin to understand why the world's main divisive issues—divided Germany, divided Korea, and divided Vietnam, to name only the most obvious— are as far from solution as they were when they first arose.

The reason power politics is now out of date is that war is unusable as an instrument of national policy. It is unusable legally, because we have made it so in the United Nations Charter. It is unusable practically, because the possible extinction of all life in the northern hemisphere that might result is, in the language of the Pentagon, unacceptable. What is not adequately understood is that, when war becomes obsolete, methods of dispute settling that depended upon the ultimate availability of war also become obsolete. Old-fashioned diplomacy was not typically an exercise in finding the intrinsic rights and wrongs of a controversy such as a boundary dispute. What the parties really were concerned about was which one could defeat the other if matters came to a military showdown. If country A could convince country B that it had decisively superior military power, the boundary would move to the disadvantage of B. But if neither could convince the other of such superiority, sooner or later there would be a military collision. One side would lose; one would win; and the process would start over again. This, somewhat simplified, has been the story of international dispute settling through most of human history.

But now something new has been added. Because of the unusability of nuclear weapons, we have a military deadlock between the great powers on the major issues. The new fact of life is that when you have military deadlock you also have diplomatic deadlock. Yet in the teeth of this observable fact, we go on trying to settle disputes by diplomacy as if we were still living in the days of Machiavelli or Metternich.

The second misconcept, closely related to the first, is that in all international situations it is power that ultimately counts. We have just seen that, as between the nuclear giants, the effect of power is not to gain advantage but to preserve a stalemate. But even as between a nuclear power and a small nation, nuclear power is virtually useless when disputes arise.

For example, at the time of the Korean conflict, the use of nuclear weapons to bring a quick end to the struggle and save the lives of thousands of American soldiers was apparently never a serious enough possibility to warrant public discussion. There is no evidence that the Soviet Union in its contest with the People's Republic of China is enjoying any advantage because of its overwhelming superiority in military strength. Poland and other satellites are taking a more independent line toward Moscow than before Russia acquired effective nuclear armaments. The awesome destructive capacity of the United States is of no use to it in relation to Cuba, and does not prevent such a humiliating episode as the Bay of Pigs invasion;

nor is nuclear strength of any relevance in South Vietnam, Malaysia, Yemen, Cyprus, the Northern India border, and the many other trouble spots in Africa, Asia, and around the world.

The third misconcept is that nations cannot bring themselves to accept settlement of their important disputes by peaceful means such as arbitration and adjudication. The fact is that nations have repeatedly submitted controversies involving high interests and high public excitement to peaceful settlement. During the nineteenth century 177 major disputes between nations were resolved by arbitration, including seventy-nine to which the United States was a party. Nor will it do to try to explain this fact away by saying that nations only submit unimportant issues to peaceful settlement. No type of controversy in international affairs is more emotion-packed than a dispute over territory. One recalls Hamlet's soliloquy about how nations will fight over a strip of ground too small to bury the dead in. Yet Norway (which was the country that prompted Hamlet's observation) gave up East Greenland to Denmark as the result of a court decision. In the last few years, boundary disputes important enough to provoke armed conflict between Nicaragua and Honduras, and between Cambodia and Thailand, have been settled in the World Court. The fact is that adjudication or arbitration on the merits is usually the only way a hotly contested boundary dispute can be settled. The reason is that no government could make a diplomatic settlement giving away the sacred soil of the motherland and still survive politically at home, but a judicial settlement reaching the same result involves no such political disaster.

The fourth misconcept is that, since there is no world government with overwhelming military power to enforce law, nations will not pay any attention to judicial or arbitral decisions that they do not like. The fact is that there is no case on record of disobedience to a decision of the Permanent Court of International Justice, and only one case of disobedience to a decision of the current International Court of Justice; and among the hundreds of other judicial and arbitral awards, there are only a few cases in which the losing party has refused to give effect to the decision. It is generally agreed by scholars that the record of compliance with international decisions compares favorably with that of compliance with domestic decisions.

When we come to the area of the peacekeeping potential of the United Nations, we encounter similarly erroneous notions. For example, it is constantly said that the usefulness of the organization is limited because it can only act when there is great-power unanimity. Yet even the most cursory look at the record shows that every major peacekeeping action of the U. N. was undertaken despite the opposition of at least one power possessed of the Security Council veto: Korea, opposed by the Soviet Union; the Middle East force, opposed and indeed vetoed by Great Britain and France in the Security Council; and the Congo action, opposed in greater or less degree by every major power except the United States.

Running through all our international misconcepts is an entire network of outdated ideas about the Soviet Union, Communism, and the cold war. One such idea is the notion that the Soviet Union never changes. The fact is that when the events in that area since the death of Stalin are seen in historical perspective it may well be concluded that Khrushchev worked a greater change in the Soviet Union than has ever been achieved without revolution in a major country in a comparable period of time. An allied fallacy is the assertion that all totalitarian regimes are alike, and that there is really no difference between today's Soviet Union and Hitler's Germany. For present purposes, there may be cited just one interesting difference. The entire force of Hitler's immense propaganda machine was devoted to preparing the German people to accept war; whereas everywhere one travels in the Soviet Union today one encounters nothing but propaganda for peace. This is not for the benefit of outsiders; this is for the home folks. This is not to ignore the problem of reconciling Russian words and policies in this area of seeking peace; the point here is merely that if the Soviet Union at some future time were to decide to plunge into the kind of flagrantly warlike course that Hitler took, it would have to reckon with a generation that, instead of having been trained to regard war as noble and inevitable, as was the case with the

Hitler youth, has been suffused with the message that war is the greatest evil, and peace the highest good for which mankind can hope.

In the same bundle of outdated notions is the idea that all conflicts in the world can ultimately be explained as Communism versus anti-Communism. It would be difficult to calculate how many blunders of policy and errors of strategy this persistent fallacy has produced and may still produce. A large part of the quarrels now going on around the world go back to animosities and rivalries that were old before Communism was even heard of: between Arabs and Jews, between Hindus and Moslems, between dozens of African tribes, between Greeks and Turks, between innumerable nations, groups, religions, and factions in all parts of the world with old scores to settle and new frictions attendant upon the decolonialization process. True, Communism is not averse to fishing in these troubled waters; but this is quite a different matter from supposing that if Communism could somehow be made to go away the world's conflicts would largely disappear.

The bipolar picture of global conflict is discredited even more decisively by the break between the Soviet Union and Communist China. It has become clear that this is no mere ideological debate. It is a dead-earnest national struggle between two natural rivals, involving the largest territorial dispute in the world, a life-and-death battle for the allegiance of a large part of the world's population, and a growing racial conflict that could dwarf any other such conflict we have yet seen, as the Communist Chinese try to mobilize racialism on a global basis.

This, then, is a mere sampling of erroneous notions that too often take the place of accurate facts in the conduct of international affairs. The list could be extended to dozens of other items, large and small. What then is to be done about this dangerous state of affairs?

The fundamental requisite is acceptance of the idea that the techniques of research, scholarship, and the scientific method have much more to contribute to the amelioration of human and international troubles than has ever been suspected. It is curious how difficult it is to get this point accepted. At one of our Soviet-American Citizens' Conferences we were trying to demonstrate that a three-man "troika" instead of a single Secretary-General of the United Nations simply would not work. Professor Louis Sohn cited a research study done at Harvard, investigating the workings of various kinds and sizes of international boards, panels, and commissions. The study showed that, of all possible bodies, the three-man group worked worst. One reason was the tendency, familiar to all seasoned committee workers, of two men in a three-man group to gang up on the third. Every triumvirate has its Lepidus and its Caesar. We reminded the Russians that they had recently had a demonstration of this phenomenon in the triumvirate that succeeded Stalin. On the other hand, a board of five or seven or nine members was found by the study to eliminate most of these kinds of difficulty. We pointed out to the Russians that if a comparable study with a comparable mass of data had shown what happens when you combine two hydrogen atoms with one oxygen atom, they would not hesitate to accept the validity of the study's findings. But merely because the subject of the study was human behavior, it is all too easy to ignore the observed facts and go on and on making the same mistakes forever.

About six years ago there was a significant turning in this entire story: the upsurge of what may be called the "peace-research movement." The central conviction of this movement is that the scholarly and research community have an important and indeed vital role to play in building the structures and procedures and attitudes that are essential to peace. The physical sciences should probably be credited with having taken the lead. At a time when, for example, inspection was the cornerstone of our disarmament position, it became apparent that no meaningful political discussion of inspection could be undertaken unless a vast amount of scientific data was developed, bearing on such obvious questions as the distance from which particular kinds of underground blasts could be detected. To continue the example of disarmament: the lawyers and economists soon saw that their disciplines also bore upon crucial points. As a matter of law, could our negotiators really promise that Russian inspectors could enter private plants in the United States even if the owners objected? As a matter of economics, could disarmament be accomplished without severe depression and unemployment?

Research centers began to be formed for the express purpose of methodically supplying the needed data and analysis. A Peace Research Committee, which produced designs for research in law, science and technology, economics, communications, and decision-making, was formed. Over 500 projects are described in these books. The Committee then led to the Peace Research Institute, Inc., with Ambassador James J. Wadsworth as its first president. Now there are active peace-research institutes and programs in dozens of countries. The new importance of research is seen in the prominent place occupied by research in the purposes and budget of the Arms Control and Disarmament Agency.

The significance of all this is that, for the first time, we are witnessing a methodical intellectual assault upon the stubborn problems, both fundamental and detailed, whose solution is a precondition to any workable and structured peace. This is not a matter of preaching peace in generalities or slogans, nor is it a matter of constructing shining models of a utopian world order. It is a matter of beginning from where we are, working with what we have and within the limits of the possible, and finding ways both to handle the day's troubles more effectively and to construct gradually better procedures, laws, and institutional arrangements for the settling of all disputes and the prevention of all threats to the peace of the world as they arise.

We'll Never Conquer Space

by Arthur C. Clarke

A British science writer injects a note of caution as men look longingly at the stars. Plans for interplanetary communication and travel are still limited by those inescapable opponents of exploration—distance and time.

Man will never conquer space. Such a statement may sound ludicrous, now that our rockets are already 100 million miles beyond the moon and the first human travelers are preparing to leave the atmosphere. Yet it expresses a truth which our forefathers knew, one we have forgotten—and our descendants must learn again, in heartbreak and loneliness.

Our age is in many ways unique, full of events and phenomena which never occurred before and can never happen again. They distort our thinking, making us believe that what is true now will be true forever, though perhaps on a larger scale. Because we have annihilated distance on this planet, we imagine that we can do it once again. The facts are far otherwise, and we will see them more clearly if we forget the present and turn our minds toward the past.

To our ancestors, the vastness of the earth was a dominant fact controlling their thoughts and lives. In all earlier ages than ours, the world was wide indeed, and no man could ever see more than a tiny fraction of its immensity. A few hundred miles—a thousand, at the most—was infinity. Only a lifetime ago, parents waved farewell to their emigrating children in the virtual certainty that they would never meet again.

And now, within one incredible generation, all this has changed. Over the seas where Odysseus wandered for a decade, the Rome-Beirut Comet whispers its way within the hour. And above that, the closer satellites span the distance between Troy and Ithaca in less than a minute.

Psychologically as well as physically, there are no longer any remote places on earth. When a friend leaves for what was once a far country, even if he has no intention of returning, we cannot feel that same sense of irrevocable separation that saddened our forefathers. We know that he is only hours away by jet liner, and that we have merely to reach for the telephone to hear his voice.

In a very few years, when the satellite communication network is established, we will be able to see friends on the far side of the earth as easily as we talk to them on the other side of the town. Then the world will shrink no more, for it will have become a dimensionless point.

But the new stage that is opening up for the human drama will never shrink as the old one has done. We have abolished space here on the little earth; we can never abolish the space that yawns between the stars. Once again we are face to face with immensity and must accept its grandeur and terror, its inspiring possibilities and its dreadful restraints. From a world that has become too small, we are moving out into one that will forever be too large, whose frontiers will recede from us always more swiftly than we can reach out towards them.

Consider first the fairly modest solar, or planetary, distances which we are now preparing to assault. The very first Lunik made a substantial impression upon them, traveling more than 200 million miles from the earth—six times the distance to Mars. When we have harnessed nuclear energy for spaceflight, the solar system will contract until it is little larger than the earth today. The remotest of the planets will be perhaps no more than a week's travel from the earth, while Mars and Venus will be only a few hours away.

This achievement, which will be witnessed within a century, might appear to make even the solar system a comfortable, homely place, with such giant planets as Saturn and Jupiter playing much the same role in our thoughts as do Africa or Asia today. (Their qualitative differences of climate, atmosphere and gravity, fundamental though they are, do not concern us at the moment.) To some extent this may be true, yet as soon as we pass beyond the orbit of the moon, a mere quarter-million miles away, we will meet the first of the barriers that will separate the earth from her scattered children.

The marvelous telephone and television network that will soon enmesh the whole world, making all men neighbors, cannot be extended into space. It will never be possible to converse with anyone on another planet.

Do not misunderstand this statement. Even with today's radio equipment, the problem of sending speech to the other planets is almost trivial. But the messages will take minutes—sometimes hours—on their journey, because radio and light waves travel at the same limited speed of 186,000 miles a second.

Twenty years from now you will be able to listen to a friend on Mars, but the words you hear will have left his mouth at least three minutes earlier, and your reply will take a corresponding time to reach him. In such circumstances, an exchange of verbal messages is possible—but not a conversation.

Even in the case of the nearby moon, the 2½-second time lag will be annoying. At distances of more than a million miles, it will be intolerable.

To a culture which has come to take instantaneous communication for granted, as part of the very structure of civilized life, this "time barrier" may have a profound psychological impact. It will be a perpetual reminder of universal laws and limitations against which not all our technology can ever prevail. For it seems as certain as anything can be that no signal—still less any material object—can ever travel faster than light.

The velocity of light is the ultimate speed limit, being part of the very structure of space and time. Within the narrow confines of the solar system, it will not handicap us too severely, once we have accepted the delays in communication which it involves. At the worst, these will amount to twenty hours—the time it takes a radio signal to span the orbit of Pluto, the outermost planet.

Between the three inner worlds, the earth, Mars, and Venus, it will never be more than twenty minutes—not enough to interfere seriously with commerce or administration, but more than sufficient to shatter those personal links of sound or vision that can give us a sense of direct contact with friends on earth, wherever they may be.

It is when we move out beyond the confines of the solar system that we come face to face with an altogether new order of cosmic reality. Even today, many otherwise educated men—like those savages who can count to three but lump together all numbers beyond four—cannot grasp the profound distinction between solar and stellar space. The first is the space enclosing our neighboring worlds, the planets; the second is that which embraces those distant suns, the stars, and it is literally millions of times greater.

There is no such abrupt change of scale in terrestrial affairs. To obtain a mental picture of the distance to the nearest star, as compared with the distance to the nearest planet, you must imagine a world in which the closest object to you is only five feet away—and then there is nothing else to see until you have traveled a thousand miles.

Many conservative scientists, appalled by these cosmic gulfs, have denied that they can ever be crossed. Some people never learn; those who sixty years ago scoffed at the possibility of flight, and ten (even five!) years ago laughed at the idea of travel to the planets, are now quite sure that the stars will always be beyond our reach. And again they are wrong, for they have failed to grasp the great lesson of our age—that if something is possible in theory, and no fundamental scientific laws oppose its realization, then sooner or later it will be achieved. " One day, it may be in this century, or it may be a thousand years from now, we shall discover a really efficient means of propelling our space vehicles. Every technical device is always developed to its limit (unless it is superseded by something better) and the ultimate speed for spaceships is the velocity of light. They will never reach that goal, but they will get very close to it. "And then the nearest star will be less than five years' voyaging from the earth.

Our exploring ships will spread outwards from their home over an ever-expanding sphere of space. It is a sphere which will grow at almost—but never quite—the speed of light. Five years to the triple system of Alpha Centauri, ten to the strangely-matched doublet Sirius A and B, eleven to the tantalizing enigma of 61 Cygni, the first star suspected to possess a planet. These journeys are long, but they are not impossible. Man has always accepted whatever price was necessary for his explorations and discoveries, *and the price of Space is Time*.

Even voyages which may last for centuries or millennia will one day be attempted. Suspended animation has already been achieved in the laboratory, and may be the key to interstellar travel. Self-contained cosmic arks which will be tiny traveling worlds in their own right may be another solution, for they would make possible journeys of unlimited extent, lasting generation after generation.

The famous Time Dilation effect predicted by the Theory of Relativity, whereby time appears to pass more slowly for a traveler moving at almost the speed of light, may be yet a third. And there are others.

Looking far into the future, therefore, we must picture a slow (little more than half a billion miles an hour!) expansion of human activities outwards from the solar system, among the suns scattered across the region of the galaxy in which we now find ourselves. These suns are on the average five light-years apart; in other words, we can never get from one to the next in less than five years.

To bring home what this means, let us use a down-to-earth analogy. Imagine a vast ocean, sprinkled with islands —some desert, others perhaps inhabited. On one of these islands an energetic race has just discovered the art of building ships. It is preparing to explore the ocean, but must face the fact that the very nearest island is five years' voyaging away, and that no possible improvement in the technique of shipbuilding will ever reduce this time.

In these circumstances (which are those in which we will soon find ourselves) what could the islanders achieve? After a few centuries, they might have established colonies on many of the nearby islands and have briefly explored many others. The daughter colonies might themselves have sent out further pioneers, and so a kind of chain reaction would spread the original culture over a steadily expanding area of the ocean.

But now consider the effects of the inevitable, unavoidable time lag. There could be only the most tenuous contact between the home island and its offspring. Returning messengers could report what had happened on the nearest colony—five years ago. They could never bring information more up to date than that, and dispatches from the more distant parts of the ocean would be from still further in the past—perhaps centuries behind the times. There would never be news from the other islands, but only history.

All the star-borne colonies of the future will be independent, whether they wish it or not. Their liberty will be inviolably protected by Time as well as Space. They must go their own way and achieve their own destiny, with no help or hindrance from Mother Earth.

At this point, we will move the discussion on to a new level and deal with an obvious objection. Can we be sure that the velocity of light is indeed a limiting factor? So many "impassible" barriers have been shattered in the past; perhaps this one may go the way of all the others.

We will not argue the point, or give the reasons why scientists believe that light can never be outraced by any form of radiation or any material object. Instead, let us assume the contrary and see just where it gets us. We will even take the most optimistic possible case and imagine that the speed of transportation may eventually become infinite.

Picture a time when, by the development of techniques as far beyond our present engineering as a transistor is beyond a stone axe, we can reach anywhere we please instantaneously, with no more effort than by dialing a number. This would indeed cut the universe down to size and reduce its physical immensity to nothingness. What would be left?

Everything that really matters. For the universe has two aspects—its scale, and its overwhelming, mind-numbing complexity. Having abolished the first, we are now face-to-face with the second.

What we must now try to visualize is not size, but quantity. Most people today are familiar with the simple notation which scientists use to describe large numbers; it consists merely of counting zeroes, so that a hundred becomes 10^2, a million, 10^6, a billion, 10^9 and so on. This useful trick enables us to work with quantities of any magnitude, and even defense-budget totals look modest when expressed as 5.76×10^9 instead of $5,760,000,000.

The number of other suns in our own galaxy (that is, the whirlpool of stars and cosmic dust of which our sun is an out-of-town member, lying in one of the remoter spiral arms) is estimated at about 10^{11}—or written in full, 100,000,000,000. Our present telescopes can observe something like 10^9 other galaxies, and they show no sign of thinning out even at the extreme limit of vision.

There are probably at least as many galaxies in the whole of creation as there are stars in our own galaxy, but let us confine ourselves to those we can see. They must contain a total of about 10^{11} times 10^9 stars, or 10^{20} stars altogether. One followed by twenty other digits is, of course, a number beyond all understanding.

Before such numbers, even spirits brave enough to face the challenge of the light-years must quail. The detailed examination of all the grains of sand on all the beaches of the world is a far smaller task than the exploration of the universe.

And so we return to our opening statement. Space can be mapped and crossed and occupied without definable limit; but it can never be conquered. When our race has reached its ultimate achievements, and the stars themselves are scattered no more widely than the seed of Adam, even then we shall still be like ants crawling on the face of the earth. The ants have covered the world, but have they conquered it—for what do their countless colonies know of it, or of each other?

So it will be with us as we spread outwards from Mother Earth, loosening the bonds of kinship and understanding, hearing faint and belated rumors at second—or third—or thousandth-hand of an ever-dwindling fraction of the entire human race.

Though Earth will try to keep in touch with her children, in the end all the efforts of her archivists and historians will be defeated by time and distance, and the sheer bulk of material. For the number of distinct societies or nations, when our race is twice its present age, may be far greater than the total number of all the men who have ever lived up to the present time.

We have left the realm of human comprehension in our vain effort to grasp the scale of the universe, so it must always be, sooner rather than later.

When you are next outdoors on a summer night, turn your head toward the zenith. Almost vertically above you will be shining the brightest star of the northern skies— Vega of the Lyre, twenty-six years away at the speed of light, near enough the point of no return for us short-lived creatures. Past this blue-white beacon, fifty times as brilliant as our sun, we may send our minds and bodies, but never our hearts.

For no man will ever turn homewards from beyond Vega, to greet again those he knew and loved on the earth.

Portrait of
Homo Aquaticus

by James Dugan

*A writer-friend of Captain Jacques-Yves Cousteau out-
lines the underwater explorer's adventures as he expands
a new frontier of science; he then suggests that man's
next move might be toward the sea, the original cradle
of life.*

The undersea explorer, Jacques-Yves Cousteau, recently made a startling proposal to the World Congress
on Underwater Activities. He told a gathering of several
hundred underwater experts that a new kind of man was
evolving—*Homo aquaticus,* who would live in the depths
of the sea. Aquatic man would dwell among his kind in
submerged towns and swim about on his daily labors in
the open depths. To permit him to travel three-dimen-
sionally beneath the waves without breathing he would un-
dergo a surgical transformation. Ultimately the new species would be born in the deep.

Cousteau's proposal did not seem far fetched to diving
physiologists and oceanographers at the meeting. It was
no surprise to the distinguished zoologist, Sir Alister Hardy,
who postulates that the human species has already gone
through an aquatic stage in its development, perhaps 60,-
000 years ago. *Homo aquaticus* would seem to be completing the cycle by returning to the sea.

I first met Captain Cousteau in 1944 in a lively London
rendezvous called Le Petit Club Français on St. James's
Place, and it now seemed an appropriate place to ask him
about his newest idea. The explorer is a lithe, long-leg-
ged man of fifty-two, with a beaked, ascetic face that often breaks into a devastating grin. One time, in the planning session of a radical new device for submarine investigation, he gave his associates pause by asking, "Well, I

think it will work and perhaps bring valuable information, but the important question is, 'Will it be fun?' "

The subject of our original wartime talk had been the Aqua-Lung, the now-famous independent automatic compressed-air diving apparatus that Cousteau had developed with the engineer, Émile Gagnan. It was the first stride in developing the underwater man that Cousteau now envisions complete.

The Aqua-Lung is a portable assembly of one or more bottles of compressed air harnessed to the diver's back and piped to a mouthpiece through the Cousteau-Gagnan regulator, which delivers air on a "demand" basis in direct response to human respiration. The regulator automatically serves the air compressed to a degree matching the pressure of the surrounding water, so that the human lungs can withstand the increase as the diver goes down and the decrease as he ascends.

The Aqua-Lung liberated underwater man from air lines to the surface. It allows three-dimensional "flights" with the essential aid of three other accouterments—the diving mask sealing off the eyes and nose, belt weights adjusting the body to neutral buoyancy, and rubber foot fins, which were also invented by a Frenchman, Yves de Corlieu.

Cousteau said:

> The Aqua-Lung came about because we wanted to stay down longer than we could by just holding our breath. The Aqua-Lung multiplied submersion time by a hundred, but the time extension let us see things that made us want to stay below much longer. I can't tell you how many times toward the end of a deep dive we have seen an unknown animal or a strange activity that we wanted to investigate further but the timekeeper above fired a warning shot into the water and we had to leave. Then, after three hours of rest before we could go down again, the strange thing was gone.
>
> Diving has gone beyond sport: it is now a worldwide movement. Science has taken it up as a prosaic tool of investigation. The imperative need now is to place swimmers underwater for very long periods to learn something about the sea. I think there will

be a conscious and deliberate evolution of *Homo aquaticus,* spurred by human intelligence rather than the slow, blind natural adaptation of species. We are now moving toward an alteration in human anatomy to give man almost unlimited freedom underwater.

Cousteau has been called "the greatest adventurer of our time." He describes himself as an "oceanographic technician." By profession he was a gunnery officer in the French Navy, from which he retired in 1957. He was born in 1910 on a sentimental maternal journey from Paris to the Gironde Department, where his father and other forebearers had been wine exporters. The child survived a painful birth and grave infant diseases. Cousteau *père* was a world-ranging businessman whose traveler's tales inspired the boy to follow suit. From the age of nine the lad spent two years in New York with his father, attended a West Side parish school, played stickball in the street and called himself "Jack."

His first underwater venture was in a New England lake, where he dove to clear sunken branches under the springboard. It aroused no interest in investigating the bottom because diving masks did not exist then to bring the submerged scenery into focus.

When masks appeared in the mid-30's, Cousteau was on navy duty at Toulon. He was semi-crippled from a gruesome sports-car crash on a foggy night in the Vosges. Surgeons had prepared to amputate his fractured left arm because of massive nerve injuries, but Cousteau refused and won back partial use of the limb by dogged physiotherapy.

At Toulon he was completing the cure by hours of ocean swimming when a shipmate, Lt. Philippe Tailliez, introduced him to the diving mask. Cousteau's first glimpse of undersea detail instantly decided his life ambition to see everything he could beneath the surface.

Without breathing apparatus, he, Tailliez and Frédéric Dumas plunged seventy feet down on held breath. To stay longer "downstairs," Cousteau and the engineer, Émile Gagnan, devised the Aqua-Lung. The invention was completed and sea-tested under precarious conditions during the Axis occupation of France and kept secret until France was liberated.

Cousteau and Dumas described their first decade with the Aqua-Lung in *The Silent World* (1953), a book that has been published in twenty-seven languages, including Russian and Icelandic. It and the Aqua-Lung set off the present boom in underwater sport and exploration. A bigger audience was drawn to free diving by Cousteau's feature film of *The Silent World*. (Before he discovered diving he wanted to be a movie-maker.) The film took a Hollywood Oscar and the Grand Prix at the 1956 Cannes International Film Festival. The producer, however, is not a man to rest on his Oscars. He promptly made a non-submersible film, *The Golden Fish,* which won another Motion Picture Academy Award for short subjects.

In 1950 Cousteau acquired a former British Navy mine sweeper, the *Calypso,* and converted her to a marine-research vessel. His *Calypso* oceanographic expeditions have ranged through many seas with new techniques of depth exploration, including a deep-sea camera sled that travels across the floor miles down making color motion pictures with synchronized electronic flash. To work up new gadgets, he founded an undersea research and development laboratory in Marseilles called the O.F.R.S. (Office Française de Recherches Sous-Marines). It produced the Diving Saucer, a two-man jet-propelled observational submarine that has taken awed scientists on dozens of voyages 1,000 feet down.

Six years ago an international committee of scientists chose Captain Cousteau to direct the Musée Océanographique in Monaco, the oldest and largest institution of its kind. He has stoutly resisted both the sedentary life of an administrator and the fashion among research establishments of accepting contracts for classified military investigations. Workers in the fifty-odd laboratories at his museum openly publish their results and those of other oceanographers in the most rapid scholarly press in existence—The Bulletin of the Musée Océanographique. Within six weeks after a scientist has checked his printed proofs, the publication is in the mail to 1,800 far-flung marine-research centers.

As befits a busy worker in hydrology, Cousteau is hydra-headed. One of his hats is that of president of the World Underwater Federation, made up of amateur divers in three dozen nations. He wears the board chairman's helmet at U. S. Divers Co. in Los Angeles, the world's largest manfuacturer of diving gear. He is one of the best customers of international airlines. His spirited wife, Simone, recently suffered a nightmare starring her spouse, in which, not having enough to occupy his time, Cousteau had taken a job as a night clerk in the Hotel Royalton in New York.

Despite his kaleidoscopic activities, Cousteau does not give an appearance of haste. He has a lively demeanor but is basically a calm and reflective man. During our recent talk his wide-ranging mind touched upon an inter-relation between research on man-in-space and man-in-the-sea. He cited an effort by U. S. space medicos to find "a sort of artificial gill in a small capsule. It would allow the astronaut to regenerate his blood with oxygen without breathing air. The 'gill' might be fitted under an arm and linked with the aorta by surgical manipulation.

"For divers, the problem is more difficult," said Cousteau. "There is also pressure to be considered. The oxygen capsule, bypassing the human lungs, would leave them subject to collapse underwater. This may be overcome by packing the rib cage with a noncompressible sterile plastic."

He added with a smile:

> Of course an even better way to produce *Homo aquaticus* would be to make a real manfish. He would inhale water instead of air just as a fish does. There would be mechanical assistance to extract oxygen from the water. There is nothing freakish about the idea. During the first nine months of hu-man life we grew while immersed in fluid in the womb. In fact, the first great crisis of life is the moment when we pass from the liquid to the air medium at birth.

Cousteau believes that the underwater species will come in about fifty years. ["He should be able to swim to a depth of about a mile, instead of the mere fifty fathoms

[300 feet] of present-day free-diving," he said. *"Homo aquaticus* won't be able to go beyond a mile because, when we reach that stratum, the external pressure will be about 170 atmospheres. At that point tissue would begin to compress and the body would be literally wrecked."

However, he felt optimistic about what could be done in the one-mile-depth range. "Virtually all the food and raw materials we could exploit on the ocean-floor area exist in this zone of the continental shelf and the continental slope," he said.

The theorist pooh-poohed the idea that it would be hard to find people willing to be altered into menfish. "You can find volunteers for everything. Look at the applicants for astronaut training and the 'human guinea pigs' in dangerous medical experiments. Man has an adventurous and inquisitive nature," said Cousteau.

He thought that the first experimental subjects would be calm, intelligent young men of twenty-five to thirty with considerable diving experience.

> They will be people who have long since lost any subjective fears of the new environment. They will *want* to spend time underwater, not merely to see *if* they can, [said Cousteau]. If I were picking them, I would look for young marine scientists with studies they wanted to carry out. Later on, the new species could be created at birth in submarine clinics with a prompt operation to "acclimatize" the babies as early as possible. The infant, with its experience in the womb just behind it, would be a natural.

Would *Homo aquaticus* spend his entire life submerged?

> Of course not, [said Cousteau]. Who would deny him the wonders of the world above? The evolutionary surgical operation would not interfere with visits to the atmosphere. The people of the deep will get a thrill out of skiing, flying, sunsets. And as technicians they will have lots of reasons for liaison with land.

But *H. aquaticus* will not be produced without a

vast increase in diving medical research. Prolonged submersion may reveal ailments that we know nothing about today.

Having seen Captain Cousteau's little jet submarine, the Diving Saucer, in operation, I asked why it could not do the deep investigations instead of a new kind of man. The Saucer has eye vision and electronic and camera vision; it has extreme maneuverability and a hydraulic claw to pick up specimens and handle tools.

Cousteau said, "No machine works as well as a man. There is a more important reason for human supremacy on the ocean floor. We must create an underwater population to help accommodate our preposterous birth rate. The sea constitutes a volume of living space many times that of the land-air environment."

Cousteau has unorthodox views on the material wealth of the sea:

> It is fashionable nowadays to talk about the "endless riches of the sea." The oceans are regarded as a sort of bargain basement. I don't agree with this estimate. The supply of food and minerals in the oceans has to be limited. Very few people are trying to harvest the sea in a rational way.

> For instance, take commercial fishing techniques. If we obtained food on land only by sending out gunners and fowlers to bag wild game, we should all be starving in short order. But the trawling system is about as primitive as that. Soon we are going to have some improvement by the use of diver-piloted nets, but this may not be much better than machine-gunning gazelles from a jeep. Whenever increase comes about in commercial fishing, the human population increase will overtake it.

Cousteau thinks the coming means in seafood production will be "farming" rather than pursuit of wild creatures:

> Ages ago man selected the most productive wild animals to domesticate—the horse for power, the

goat and cow for milk, the chicken for eggs, and all of them—plus the pig—for edible flesh.

Stock-farming is the logical next stage in the sea. That is one of the biggest reasons for *Homo aquaticus.* He will select the likeliest animals for domestication underwater. Today, we cultivate only shellfish and seaweed in tidal shallows. When we go deeper, to ranch on the open range, selections of the most productive food species will vary and enrich our diet. We may be eating sea slugs as the Chinese do. We may find that the ideal ranch animal is not a finned fish but an enormous marine worm that accumulates edible protein faster than any fish.

The undersea villagers that Cousteau foresees will reside in dry, gas-filled houses on the bottom and live pretty much like householders on shore. But their workday will be spent in the water.

Last autumn two men of his diving team, Albert Falco and Claude Wesly, remained underwater for a week, residing in a seventeen-foot cylinder, eight feet in diameter. It was supplied with air compressed to equal that of the sea outside and the men went out in the water with Aqua-Lungs to work five hours a day. The project, called Continental Shelf Station No. 1, showed that men could adapt to such a life and that extended submersion afforded them observations of terrain and fish behavior denied to episodic free divers. Cousteau said, "In future Continental Shelf Stations we intend to go longer and deeper with more people."

I asked Cousteau if his colonies of underwater workers would be active in submarine mining.

This possibility is being exaggerated, [he said]. Although Peter Keeble and Sammy Collins are mining diamonds with a suction pipe on the western continental shelf of South Africa, I must say I'm pessimistic about a bonanza of raw materials from the sea. The work is difficult and too expensive to bear out rosy predictions. The sea isn't going to give us anything without a hard struggle and vast capital outlays. However, the day may be coming when we shall need whatever minerals can be taken below, and to that extent, yes, the undersea colony will do the job better than groping from the surface.

Cousteau's London talk on *Homo aquaticus* did not meet with unanimous approval. An official of the congress dismissed his forecast as "science fiction" and placed his faith in mechanical progress in submarine exploration. I asked Cousteau what he thought about that.

What's wrong with science fiction as a presentiment of reality? [he asked]. Ever since Jules Verne, and lots of people before him, the informed human imagination has projected what is to come. Actually, I was trying to be conservative in talking about the underwater future in London. Why, there were people there who wanted to talk about milking whales in regular underwater dairies!

The undersea explorer said:

At the underwater congress a man asked me what *Homo aquaticus* would expect to find under the sea that we have not discovered already. The question was fairly breathtaking. We know practically nothing about the depths of the ocean!

I was reminded of something Harold Edgerton said to a similar question. He was working around the bathyscaphe in Toulon, fitting one of his electronic-flash depth cameras for a 5,000-foot dive. A promenader said, "Ah, the Kodak for sharks! Tell me, what do you expect to photograph down there?" Edgerton said, "Brother, if I knew, I wouldn't bother trying." Science does not work on predictable goals. The word "science" merely means knowledge. *Homo aquaticus* will be created for the pursuit of knowledge, not just to farm fish or collect manganese.

"To me, the coming undersea life will be *inspiriting*. I don't mean spiritually or religiously, but a life full of daily inspiration like that to which man has risen as a result of creative developments in his past—the Greek concept of the ethos, the High Renaissance, the eighteenth-century revolutions. Their echoes form the best in our lives today. I think undersea man will have the purest of these adventures."

"Science, Life, and Landscape"
by Paul B. Sears

An ecologist traces man's development as a biological and social being and concludes that, though a limited number of men may explore the sea, the majority must continue to meet the problem of sustaining life by proper management of the land. He feels the solution lies with the creative artist whose vision is expanded through science.

"Thou canst not stir a flower without troubling of a star"
So sang Francis Thompson, the British poet. Affirming the unity of the world of nature, his artistic intuition had been clarified by the Darwinian revolution in human thought. For Darwin, in demonstrating the infinitely long course in evolutionary process, had shown that environment and life, including that of mankind, were inseparable components of a greater whole.

What the plodding, thoughtful Darwin, whose poor scholastic record would have barred him from a modern graduate school, had done, was to revive a belief long lost to Western thought. This belief, implicit in ancient nature-worship, was in the kinship of man and other living things. And by a curious contradiction, it had been sacrificed when Abraham substituted the ram for his beloved son Isaac, affirming his belief in a single just God, ruling the universe by law, but reserving for man a place aloof from the rest of nature.

The faiths, Moslem and Christian, which stemmed from this break with pagan naturalism, merely intensified the sense of man's apartness and special privilege. Accretions to the simple teachings of Jesus pictured this world of mortal man as a place of tears and trial, to be got through somehow in hope of something much better, in fear of something much worse.

Centuries later the opening up of new continents with seemingly inexhaustible resources did nothing to dampen the belief of Western culture that nature could be used as man willed. There was nothing to nurture the ethic long before expressed in Taoist doctrine of the Orient, that violence toward nature is an evil, even as violence toward fellowman. Nor was the situation helped by a break with the insistence of the medieval Church that economic activities should be subordinate to ethical considerations.

This break was formalized by Adam Smith in his principle of *laissez-faire,* which proclaimed that by each serving his own selfish ends, the greatest good for all would ensue. The land and its resources came to be regarded as simple chattels, to be used or used up at the owner's caprice. Even the destruction of feudalism had its effects, for whatever the evils of that system, it was a pattern of obligation in which land, however badly it might be managed, was an object of stewardship.

The impact of Europe upon the Americas was in many ways disastrous. To begin with, agricultural reforms that had begun in the Netherlands had not reached either Great Britain or Spain at the time of colonization. In Virginia and New England, and westward from both, soil was too often regarded as a mere commodity. On the other hand, in the mid-Atlantic states, settled from the Continent, it was properly managed and conserved.

As for Spain, she had failed to preserve the practices of the thrifty and enlightened Moors and in her settlement of the New World was mostly concerned with the search for gold and silver. Only where these were lacking, as in Costa Rica and the Argentine, were farmers seriously colonized.

An additional factor operated in what is now the United States of America. Her founders, desperately fearing the development of a privileged landed class, enacted early legislation that made it all but impossible for land to be retained indefinitely in family ownership. Thus was removed the incentive, so notable even in modern France, for individuals to husband their holdings for the benefit of their descendants.

An Ohio farm in which I have life interest is a case in point. Its ownership cannot be controlled later than twenty-one years after the death of my son. My grandson will be a sturdy character indeed if he resists the temptation to get all he can while the getting is good, regardless of what happens to the land. Incidentally, but significantly, the abstract of title to this land shows that it changed hands no less than twelve times during the first twenty years after the Indians were driven from it. I would gladly right the injustice to them if it were in my power to do so.

Meanwhile I am taking the fullest possible advantage of scientific management to make this farm productive, but receiving far less than an equivalent investment in sound industry would yield. I must compete with land being opened up to irrigation by government subsidies ranging from 500 dollars to 2,500 dollars an acre in a time of surplus!

But let us return to the role of science as it affects the landscape. This is not by any means a simple matter. We date the official birth of modern science from the work of Sir Francis Bacon, sometime Lord Chancellor to Elizabeth I. This was followed presently by the influence of the agricultural reform that started in the Lowlands. During the late seventeenth and eighteenth centuries land use and management, joined with an amateur interest in science, became respectable, even fashionable, in England.

The rapid development of biology, followed by the twin birth of modern chemistry and physiology about the time of the American Revolution, intensified and refined this vogue of interest in agriculture and the land—a trend which has continued to the present day. We now have superbly trained and magnificently equipped researchers in agricultural fields. In such fashion has one of the most ancient and complex of arts been infused with the benefits of modern science. As proof of this, we need cite only the increased level of production which has created the present, if temporary, surplus on North American farms.

Yet the influence of advancing science upon the landscape has been a mixed blessing. Let us examine some of its effects. The humane application of science from the highest motives has reduced the death rate and prolonged the human life-span, without significant effect upon the birth rate. The mathematics of this situation are simple enough. The habitable earth, though vast, is finite in area and variable from place to place in its capacity to sustain populations. Sooner or later the present rate of human increase, which has no precedent in history, must tax both food supply and living space. But long before this can happen, there will be a tragic loss in the freedom of the individual.

The certainty of this rests upon sheer physical principle. For whenever the number of dynamic particles, be they molecules or men, increases within a limited space, the mean free path of each is constricted. Where people are concerned, too great a concentration brings unemployment—more workers than jobs. It also brings the grim alternative of regimentation or disorder. If one takes cities as an example, economic studies such as those of Joseph Spengler show that after the most favorable size is reached, further growth costs more than it produces. Chambers of Commerce, whose leaders should understand simple accounting, continue to ignore this fact and do all they can to promote what they call "growth." There is a vast difference between growth and health.

But physical principle goes still further. If one increases the energy within a closed system of dynamic particles, pressure is further increased, as we learn from heating a flask of gases. Since the beginning of this century the use of fossil energy in the internal-combustion engine has enormously multiplied the activity of human beings. Speed of motion and communication has been multiplied at least a thousand percent, to say nothing of the resources drawn upon and dissipated in the form of consumer goods, and the stable surface of the landscape which is being altered.

Man, a biological organism, has at length become a major geological force. This was pointed out clearly in a long-neglected book by Samuel Perkins Marsh, *Man and Nature,* first published in 1866. And Marsh, a traveler and observer of wide experience, also noted that many, if not most, of the changes which man had produced on the landscape were such as to lower its capacity to sustain his activities and those of life in general. He had seen, for example, the ruins of former mighty empires in the Mediterranean region, now marked by desolate surroundings. Correctly he saw that this was due to disruption of natural processes rather than climatic changes, as other and later students were to claim. It is well to recall that these tragedies took place long before the day of the bulldozer.

The damage to man's habitat has been intensified as science has led to the increased pressure of numbers and mechanisms. It is not due to the increase in scientific knowledge *per se,* but rather to the failure to understand and use the entire range of knowledge we have. We use science unscientifically, selecting its applications for immediate convenience and profit, rather than for its true purpose, which is to give us perspective on the system of which we are inevitably a part.

The very results of science with which we are surrounded, not to say smothered, have broken the intimate contact between the urban majority and the patterns of the natural world which control the destiny of mankind. The brilliant achievements, particularly of physical science, have led to a new and dangerous superstition—the faith that technology can preserve us from any scrape we get into. Many view technology as a way of using natural law to defeat its own inexorable operation. We might call this a superstition of the sophisticated urbanite. I doubt if it is shared by the average farm lad, or by those who go down to the sea in ships, for these are daily reminded of the forces of nature.

This widespread fallacy is not to be dispelled by expressions of opinion and warning, no matter how soundly they may be based. Rather we must look at the record, recent and ancient. We have by this time had enough experience with elaborate chains of technology to know that the greater our dependence upon them, the more vulnerable we become to the slightest failure. New York has more than once been thrown into confusion by power failure, and one can easily imagine what would happen to Los Angeles should there be any mischance in the two-hundred-mile pipeline which brings its supply of fresh water.

But let us examine an infinitely longer record, the history of the earth and its inhabitants. The known antiquity of our planet has expanded vastly from Bishop Ussher's modest estimate of 4004 B.C., and even from Lord Kelvin's judgment, based on his knowledge of physics, that the earth was not much more than twenty millions of years old. Today our closest estimates approach five billions of years.

This is twice the age of the oldest known fossils, and at least five thousand times the earliest known evidence of mankind.

The lesson is clear. An infinitely long time has been required to fit the earth for man and to develop him into the organism which he is. During that time life and landscape have become bound together, yet it is clear from the record that while man cannot survive without a suitable environment, this environment, the living landscape, can get along very well without man!

During the near-million years of his existence, the human being has changed physically in no important respect. He is first of all fitted by his physical nature and needs to his surroundings and by their ability to sustain him. What has changed is his culture. He has evolved, not by change in bodily form and function, but by developing new ways and new values to sanction them. So that over and above sheer physical bonds he is related to environment by his actions and beliefs.

For his physical survival man requires food and other organic materials, elaborated by green plants using the energy of sunlight. He also requires pure water and air as well as space for wholesome living. Like other animals he needs exercise, recreation and play to maintain reasonable vigor. These needs, as well as all biological experience, suggest that he will have to adjust his numbers to the capacity of his environment, for science knows of no instance in which any organism can increase indefinitely, without coming to terms with physical limitations. If man is an exception, he is truly a remarkable one.

So far as physical survival is involved, food has been the traditional concern, with water, air, and space taken more or less for granted. Even today attempts to estimate the carrying power of the earth deal largely with food. While its production could be increased greatly, there are hordes of people in crowded lands who live at or below a subsistence level, with the hovering threat of famine never far away. Technology, economics, and politics have not yet solved the problem of distribution.

So greatly has our modern life increased the per capita consumption of water for irrigation, industry and domestic use, in the face of increasing numbers of consumers, that adequate water supply has become a political issue, no longer a matter of theory. Although the surgeon-general of the United States has called stream pollution a national disgrace, it still goes on and efforts to clean up our rivers meet with many obstacles. Meanwhile municipalities, states, and even nations struggle for control of adequate water supplies.

One can live longer without food than without water, and longer without water than when deprived of air fit to breathe. Yet precisely where people are most densely settled the air is becoming steadily worse from industrial waste and engine fumes. Our technology is much more concerned with the elaboration of consumer goods than with the protection of what have always been considered free goods—water and air.

Food, water, and air. This leaves space—a more complicated matter, important for both physical and cultural reasons. Primitive hunters sometimes required several square miles per person to provide food enough. Agriculture changed that, and technology still more. Ohio, crowded when fifteen thousand Indians lived there, now has a population nearing ten million. It does not feed them from its own land, though it might do so in a pinch if people became vegetarians. The Megalopolis along the Atlantic seaboard could not possibly feed its own millions.

I have stated the principle governing pressure of numbers on space, with its attendant loss of freedom. Since freedom is itself a cherished cultural value, let us turn to the question of man's cultural needs. These, to a large degree, perhaps almost wholly, are set by the values of his own group.

Life in Hawaii has been enriched by the contribution of its different cultural groups. We need only mention the tradition of exquisite beauty from the Orient, the love of sunshine, music, and water of the Hawaiians. Life here, despite its activity, seems free from the grimness so evident on much of the mainland.

On the mainland some of the Osage and Navajo measure merit by the number of ponies or other livestock, and by the ability to give, rather than to get. Our leading philanthropists generally acquire this latter value late in life, but even so it is good they do for then they have the wealth to dispense.

In spite of differences, however, one common thread seems to me to run through the value systems of all cultures. This is the imperative need for some kind of certainty and confidence. The world as known by any group must somehow be made to hang together, and every culture has its own internal logic directed toward this end. Only by getting inside of any culture, so to speak, is there any hope of understanding it.

Too harsh a judgment has been passed on the early missionaries, I am convinced, for limiting the association of their children with those of the natives. Had they not respected the humanity of the Hawaiians, they would not have been here. But they could not throw off the chilling effects of one of St. Paul's least admirable views on human behavior in the face of a freer, more natural and—who knows—perhaps a more moral one.

Thus each of us finds his certainties in the values cherished by his culture, though outsiders may regard these as superstitions. It is the merit of science to have added a new dimension to our certainty—confidence in the operation of natural law. Our mistake has been to confine this new confidence to the laboratory and industrial plant, to health and agriculture, without seeing that it operates in the broader context of man's impact on the landscape. Here, as truly as in experimental fields, the chemist's test tube or bacterial cultures, the stern laws of balance operate.

I listened with respect and attention to the gallant speech of our young President [Kennedy] on the State of the Union. While I have a strong sense of the political and economic facts of life, I listened as a biologist and not as one who wished to make capital, pro or con, of his remarks. To do this was not an exhilarating experience, I assure you. For in all of the problems—unemployment, conflicts of interest, delinquency, to name but a few—I could not help sense the relentless and cumulative trend that comes from pressure of humanity on a finite landscape. Andrew Jackson is reported to have said of his population of thirteen million in 1830 that "unemployment, that ancient specter of the human race, is now forever banished." Nothing is clearer than the fact that unemployment, idle hands with too few jobs, is a function of overpopulation quite as much as lack of ingenuity.

Conflicts of interest result and become more acute as the space available to each individual lessens; delinquency and disease are the offspring of crowding. This is not to say that the United States is now overpopulated so far as its ability to support people is concerned. But the pressure of numbers has reached the point where conventional political measures deal mostly with symptoms and are pallative at best. Only by tackling the truly central problem is there hope of serving our belief in the dignity and importance of the individual.

That this involves planning is clear. Planning must be on two fronts—our rate of population increase and our most efficient use of space. Both are extremely delicate matters. Under our system the only hope of solution lies in the development of an informed public opinion of good will. Both science and the historical record agree that the satisfaction of physical and cultural needs involves an harmonious adjustment between man and the landscape. And modern social science has shown that the only hope of such an adjustment lies in the shaping of our cultural values.

This, then, is the problem toward which I have been driving. A healthy and enduring relationship between man and landscape must come by adjustment to the rules of the game, not by trying to change them. We know better than to try to squelch a volcano or blow back a hurricane. We forget that the slower and quieter operations of nature are just as relentless. Our only hope of getting along with them is by fitting our plans, our operations and our values to them. This, in technical terms, means that we must modify our culture.

Every culture has its own momentum, not easily turned aside or altered. Yet cultures do change. And change comes when individuals begin to look at themselves and their surroundings in new ways. For it is profoundly true that the actions of men and societies are governed by the kind of world in which they think they are living. The cynic thinks that every man has his price, the evangelist that every man has an immortal soul. The believer in democracy is sustained by a faith that, given the facts and a choice, the majority will generally make the better decision. Observe the basis of this—*given the facts*.

This goes much deeper than merely posting or proclaiming the facts. It is notorious that people are poisoned because they so often fail to read labels and directions, or swindled because they do not read the fine print on contracts. Facts do no good unless they become part of our thinking and doing apparatus. To affect a culture they must infuse and permeate society itself. They must be like the rain which soaks into the rich absorbent forest floor, not that which falls upon a tin roof.

Quite briefly, we must begin by trying to produce a society that is scientifically literate, without sacrifice of the humane aspects of training and learning. It is true that we are moving slowly in this direction, discussing, organizing committees and lavishing treasure, but remaining vastly confused by our obsession with gadgetry and specialization. We stereotype the scientist according to a pattern set by the graduate schools and, in my judgment, the influence sifts down and corrupts the experience with science at all levels.

To cite a single, but by no means solitary, example: When it was suggested to a prominent scientist, commissioned to work with a group trying to improve the teaching of science, that perhaps he ought to get some firsthand experience at teaching undergraduates, he snorted, "I have my graduate students. Don't think I'm going to waste my time on a lot of beginners."

In refreshing, but all too rare, contrast, let me cite the experience of Professor Frank Griffin of Reed College: In 1936–37 he took over a section of mathematics freshmen in the U.S. Grant High School of Portland, Oregon. This section was composed of the least qualified ten or twelve percent—twenty-four students who had all had trouble with grade-school arithmetic and were mostly classified as low I.Q.

Starting with easy material which they could understand and which they could see was useful, he tried to draw ideas and working rules from the youngsters themselves. He wrote on the board homework assignments that carried out classroom developments and eleven times during the year (by his report) the youngsters shouted for longer assignments. Before the year was over his group got algebra problems fully as tough as any of the regular algebra classes. Besides this they got a substantial unit on experimental geometry and some simple work on numerical trigonometry and four-place logarithms.

Such pioneering, I am happy to report, is now being brilliantly followed up and the teaching of mathematics is undergoing a revolution. So, I trust, is the secondary-school teaching in other sciences. But my concern at this time is not so much with the individual sciences, as with the general pattern or curriculum of all experience with science. Proficiency in any one is good, but if science is to have the impact on our culture which I have outlined, it must convey a balanced picture of the world of nature as we are now able to understand it. To the best of my knowledge this is now being accomplished in some of the small democracies of Western Europe, but scarcely with us.

Science involves both observation and communication. Experience with it should begin with the learning of the mother tongue. The world is full of endless interest to the growing child if we encourage and guide his curiosity instead of stifling it. Were only his future enjoyment at stake, he would still deserve the training of his senses as well as his tongue. And as he moves on through the elementary grades he should have, if we cherish our dreams, teachers who are not overburdened hacks, but who have the leisure and talent to give him some measure of personal attention. For good teaching is above all a highly personal affair.

Still thinking of pattern rather than particulars, no doubt various solutions are possible. Until something more tangible turns up, I suggest no less than four years of science in high school and two in college for an understanding of today's world.

I would further suggest that in high school, we begin with the earth and the system of which it is part. There are few satisfactions greater than reading the story of mountains, rocks, rivers, and seas, observing and respecting the forces they represent. Happily this idea is now being put into practice in Pennsylvania, although geology remains a closed book in most places.

Next I would proceed to the study of living things—organisms alive, familiar, and visible to the naked eye, reserving the microscope until it becomes a privilege instead of a penalty. And last, after there is some perspective on the larger whole, seems to me the time for chemistry and physics, for which earlier mathematics, taught as it could be, is proper preparation.

In college, for those who go there, I would be inclined to reverse this order. Taking two years, worked out as a close-knit unit and taught by men and women who believe in it, I would devote the first to a study of time, space, motion, and matter. This combination of physics and chemistry would call for sacrifice of the current idea that the first course should exist to prepare the small percentage of future specialists for the next course head.

The second year I would give over to a study of the earth and its inhabitants, again close-knit and building upon the experience of the previous year. Only those who have had the privilege of teaching the natural sciences to groups that understand physical principles will appreciate the resulting satisfactions to all concerned.

In short, the present pick-and-try of requiring a single science never was a very convincing experience, and has failed miserably to produce an educated public that is scientifically literate, with a balanced view of the world of nature. It has long outlived whatever usefulness it had.

I have tried to be as brief and painless as possible in bringing up what the late Sherlock Gass once called "the intolerable subject of education." But our problem is more complex than in the days when the classics formed a basis of common discourse among educated men. The United States Constitution, framed by men who, however they might disagree, could understand each other, is a shining tribute to the effectiveness of that older phase of intellectual history. We are grateful for the fact that these men shared an appreciation of historical process.

Today we must add, not substitute, a similar measure of common understanding of scientific process and perspective. Government with the consent of the governed also implies their participation. Wise decisions can neither be made nor enforced by any other means. More than this, if we are to reshape our culture to insure its permanence, all ranges of talent within it must be drawn upon.

To reorganize life and operation within even that simplest natural unit, the river basin, requires the collaboration of engineer, lawyer, scientist, artisan, politician, and artist, to name but a few. And cooperation is not possible among those who cannot communicate from a basis of common understanding.

Since the role of the engineer is so obvious, we may take him as an illustration. He is generally recruited from one of the highest intelligence brackets in our schools, and severely disciplined in responsibility. While his professional training is being broadened at some of the better schools, it still leaves him in many cases without any background in biology and geology, not to mention esthetics. Even were he so qualified, the manner of his employment seldom gives him freedom to do more than concentrate on his immediate responsibility, leaving to others its broader consequence. Only when he, his employers and co-workers in various fields share the kind of scientific literacy I have in mind—plus a concern for the common welfare that comes from humane education—can we hope for the fullest benefit of engineering talent.

Like engineering, the legal profession has great responsibilities, and possibilities, too, in our neotechnical age. Yet a few years ago, when it was discovered that only about one in seven Yale undergraduates took any more than the minimum science requirements, much of the trouble was traced back to freshmen counselors, most of whom were law students. Their advice was to stay away from science. It may be also that the science requirement itself was not always overappetizing.

I should like to conclude with emphasis on the vital importance of another calling, whose significance is often overlooked—sometimes I fear by those who pursue it. I refer to the artist, whatever his medium of expression may be. It is an old and neglected saying that "I care not who writes the laws of a country, so long as I can sing its songs." Like many aphorisms, this can be read in more than one way.

The simplest rendering would be "Let me alone to do

as I wish." I have no quarrel with the utmost freedom of experimentation or self-expression for any artist. Much of the sort of thing that goes on in modern music, poetry, and painting represents intense intellectual effort and technical skill. Jackson Pollock's "Forest Fire" for example I found to be a remarkable abstraction of essentials, but only because he had been thoughtful enough to label it. Otherwise I would merely have found it a curious and interesting bit of brush-weaving. On the other hand I recall the remark of a visiting French architect who said, "The artist concerned to do nothing but express himself is not necessarily a criminal, but he shares that quality with the criminal."

Beyond self-expression, many of our artists do recognize a further obligation. This is to reflect and interpret the current mood and trend. Oscar Jacobson, the Oklahoma painter, revisiting his native Europe during the 1920's, saw impending social revolution in the paintings. Ten years later we listened with disbelief to another Oklahoma colleague, back from Switzerland, where he had been born, when he said, "There are only two philosophies with any power on the continent today, naziism and communism."

When I see what I take to be the efforts of many artists today to catch and reflect our culture, I am not, nor perhaps am I supposed to be, uplifted. I find a kind of fatalism, a sense of abdication before our new masters, the machines we have ourselves created. There seems to be far more attention to the random paths of molecules and the Principle of Uncertainty than to vitality and resolution through orderly growth into true organic form. Cancer seems to have a charm that healthy tissue does not possess.

Yet our choice is plainly between despair and the struggle to achieve health. I have always thought that to be a truly great artist one must first of all be a truly great person, not wholly the victim of the contemporary scene, but gifted with hope and vision for the future. As the role of science is to minimize the range of uncertainties, so I view the role of the arts as a charge to comprehend, interpret, and dramatize the certainties and their promise.

Where there is no vision the people perish. Science has enormously enlarged our vision, but it will become our common heritage only as it is made manifest by the creative artist. Those triplet daughters of Philosophy—Ethics, Esthetics, and Logic—must walk hand in hand in the full light of knowledge to guide us.

I am indebted to Professor Norris [Ben Norris, Professor of Art, University of Hawaii], who has given profound thought to the issues raised concerning art, for comments that may clarify the situation. Recognizing, as I do also, that the symbolisms of science, are, and criticism must always be, in a sense, incommensurable, he points out that genuine abstract art is a striving for a new mystique to express the vastly widened horizons of our new knowledge.

It is interesting to note that the physicist [J. Robert] Oppenheimer believes that even within the field of science itself the various branches have passed the point of no return so far as any complete intercommunication is concerned. And apropos of my mention of cancer, the late Dr. Alan Gregg in one of his last addresses stated that the only thing to which he could compare the present unregulated multiplication of mankind was the behavior of cancer cells. Since Dr. Gregg had devoted his life to the public-health work of the Rockefeller Foundation, his humane compassion admits of no doubt.

But in speaking of the artist as translator and dramatizer of the scientific view, I had in mind simple fundamentals, long known and capable of simple expression, yet largely ignored. Because they so obviously affect the future of mankind, it is my concern that they become more generally appreciated and woven into contemporary knowledge and values. And for this task I regard the artist as essential. But this is no one-shot job. A long time has passed since Goya so clearly symbolized the horrors of warfare.

Biographical Notes

John Ciardi is one of America's most prominent poets and an articulate speaker and teacher in the field of poetry. He wrote his prize-winning first volume, *Homeward to America,* when he was twenty-three. His *How Does a Poem Mean* is a widely used text. Presently he is poetry editor for *Saturday Review,* for which he writes a regular column, "Manner of Speaking." He is also a popular lecturer at universities and at the Breadloaf Writers' Conference in Vermont.

Arthur C. Clarke graduated from the University of London after serving in the Royal Air Force during World War II. With a distinguished background in physics and mathematics, he became a science editor and later a freelance writer. Best known for his writing in the field of space conquest, he has also written short stories, novels, and radio and television scripts. Among his nonfiction works is *The Exploration of Space.*

James Dugan is the secretary of the U. S. Liaison Committee for Oceanographic Research. He wrote the text for Cousteau's movie, *The Silent World,* and is the author of *Man Under the Sea, The Great Iron Ship,* and a biography of Hans Isbrandtsen, *American Viking.* Mr. Dugan organized an underwater photographing expedition to film the sunken *Andrea Doria.*

Paul Engle is a widely known poet and teacher, serving as the director of the writers' workshop at the State University of Iowa. He edits the annual collection, *Prize Stories of America,* and is the editor of a recent book, *On Creative Writing.*

Leonard Feinberg is professor of English at Iowa State

College. He was recently Fulbright Professor of American Literature at the University of Ceylon.

Edward Morgan Forster was educated at King's College, Cambridge, and lived some years in both India and Italy. After returning to England, he served both as a critic and a literary editor for the London *Daily Herald*. He is most famous for his novels, *Where Angels Fear to Tread, A Room with a View, Howard's End,* and *A Passage to India*. He has also written two nonfiction books dealing with literature, *Abinger Harvest* and *Aspects of the Novel*. In addition to his writing, he has lectured at Cambridge and at various other universities.

Martin Gardner writes a monthly math game column for the *Scientific American* and has written several science and mathematics books for young adults. He is interested in literature as well, and has produced *The Annotated Alice* and *The Annotated Ancient Mariner*.

Harry Golden is the editor of *The Carolina Israelite*, a Jewish newspaper he began in Charlotte, North Carolina, in 1947. In addition to writing and editing everything for his newspaper, he has done an informal study of his friend, poet Carl Sandburg. His personal journalistic essays have been published in such collections as *Only in America, For 2¢ Plain, Enjoy, Enjoy!, You're Entitle',* and *The Harry Golden Omnibus*.

Robert Graves has taught English literature at Oxford University, Trinity College, and the Egyptian University. He makes his home on the island of Majorca, where he owns a jazz club. A poet and novelist, his verse collections include *Goliath and David, The Penny Fiddle: Poems for Children,* and *The Treasure Box*. His immensely popular historical novels are *I, Claudius* and *Claudius the God*. *Goodbye to All That* is an autobiography recording Mr. Graves' World War I experiences.

Tyrone Guthrie established the repertory company of the Tyrone Guthrie Theater in Minneapolis. He has staged many plays, both of the classic and contemporary worlds, and is famous for his movie adaptation of *Oedipus Rex*.

David Karp is a noted television writer and novelist whose best-known books are *One*, which has been dramatized twice for use on television, and *The Day of the Monkey*. Working for television since 1950, he has written for a number of the most popular television series.

John Keats is a critic of current society whose particular interest lies in education. His *The Sheepskin Psychosis* deals with the effects of mass higher education upon America. His *The Insolent Chariots* deals with the automobile industry. In addition to his book-length works, Mr. Keats writes a monthly column for *Holiday* and contributes to such other periodicals as *Life*, *Saturday Evening Post*, and *The New York Times Magazine*.

Jack Kerouac is an essayist, short-story writer, and novelist who is perhaps the most prominent of the "beat" writers. His novels include *The Dharma Bums*, *The Subterraneans*, *Doctor Sax*, *Maggie Cassidy*, and *On the Road*. "Alone on a Mountaintop" is part of his book, *Lonesome Traveler*.

Joseph Wood Krutch is an eminent essayist, best known for his literary criticism and nature writing. His titles include *Experience and Art*, *American Drama Since 1918*, *Five Masters*, *Samuel Johnson*, *If You Don't Mind My Saying So*, and a book about Poe, *A Study in Genius*. Mr. Krutch has also served as drama critic for *The Nation* and as columnist for the *American Scholar*.

Oliver La Farge was a novelist, an archaeologist, and a specialist in American Indian problems. His Pulitzer prize-winning *Laughing Boy* is a novel of Navajo Indian life. His other books include the autobiographical *Raw Material*, *All the Young Men*, *The Eagle in the Egg*, and his last book, *Reflections on Growing Old*.

Arthur Larson is a university professor and former Rhodes Scholar who has served as the dean of the University of Pittsburgh School of Law, Undersecretary of Labor, and director of the United States Information Agency. He is also a composer of instrumental music and an author. His books include *Design for Research in International Rule of Law* and *Preventing World War III*. He was the 1960 winner of the World Peace Award.

Russell Lynes is the author of *A Surfeit of Honey,* a study of the effect of wealth upon American life. He is a columnist for *Harper's,* where his opinions on the current American social and artistic scene reach a wide audience.

Archibald MacLeish has served as Librarian of Congress and as Undersecretary of State. He has twice received the Pulitzer prize for poetry, and his verse drama, *J.B.,* a modern retelling of the Book of Job, was a distinguished Broadway success.

Marya Mannes has been a feature editor for *Vogue* and a contributor to a wide variety of periodicals. Her subjects range from freedom of speech to freedom from the dress designers. Her book-length works include *Subverse,* a book of verse; *More in Anger,* articles and essays; *Message from a Stranger,* a novel; *The New York I Love;* and *But Will It Sell?*

Margaret Mead is a leading American anthropologist who has added significantly to the understanding of the individual and of societies through her lectures and such books as *Coming of Age in Samoa, Growing Up in New Guinea, Male and Female* and *Growth and Culture: A Photographic Study of Balinese Childhood.*

Lillian Ross is an editor and writer who has been a staff member of *The New Yorker* and a contributor of many articles to the magazine. She has spent most of her adult life in New York, where she has been associated with leading figures of our century. Her first book of fiction was *Vertical and Horizontal.* She has also written a series of fifty-five portraits of actors, with Helen Ross, called *The Player.* Seven of her best journalistic essays were collected in a volume called *Reporting.*

Paul B. Sears is an ecologist and conservationist who has written and spoken widely on the problems of man in his setting of the natural world. He was for many years chairman of Yale's conservation program and has served as Carnegie visiting professor of botany at the University of Hawaii.

Adlai E. Stevenson was the grandson of a Vice-President of the United States. Mr. Stevenson was assistant to the Secretary of the Navy during World War II, assistant to the Secretary of State and a U. S. delegate to the United Nations, a governor of Illinois, and twice a Democratic Presidential candidate. At the time of his death in London, he was acting as U. S. Ambassador to the United Nations. Collections of his essays and speeches include *Major Campaign Speeches by Adlai E. Stevenson, Call to Greatness,* and *Friends and Enemies.*

Deems Taylor combined careers in composing and criticism. His operas, *The King's Henchman* and *Peter Ibbetson,* have been performed at the Metropolitan Opera. He served as music critic for New York newspapers and as editor for *Musical America.* Two of his books are *Of Men and Music* and *The Well-tempered Listener.* He was the editor of *A Treasury of Gilbert and Sullivan.*

Arnold Toynbee is an English historian and educator who has, since 1925, acted as director of studies in London's Royal Institute of International Affairs. His *Study of History* has proved to be a best-seller among history books.